SIX APPEAL

Six Appeal

The latest and funniest compilation from *The Herald Diary*

Ken Smith and David Belcher

MAINSTREAM
PUBLISHING
EDINBURGH AND LONDON

First published in Great Britain in 2004 by
MAINSTREAM PUBLISHING COMPANY (EDINBURGH) LTD
7 Albany Street
Edinburgh EH1 3UG

ISBN 1 84018 939 8

Reprinted 2004

A catalogue record for this book is available from the British Library

Typeset in Comic Sans and Janson
Printed and bound in Great Britain by
Mackays of Chatham plc

Contents

INTRODUCTION

ONE of our proud achievements at the Diary desk in *The Herald* stems from the Scots accountant who contacted us from Germany. When he worked in Scotland, he felt himself a bit of a dull chap – never cracking a joke, never much of a hit with the ladies. Then, after transferring abroad, he read The Diary online every day, and usually found a story with which to regale the rest of the staff when they went for a stein of beer after work. Suddenly, he was the life and soul without ever saying where his tales funny and strange came from, and he wanted to thank us for helping him to find a new girlfriend. That is really what most people want – something to smile about at the end of the working day, although we cannot guarantee a new girlfriend. This sixth collection of The Diary's daily drollery is intended as a portable, ever-ready means of banishing gloom and raising flagging spirits. But like one of those awards ceremonies on the telly, we have to say thanks. A big thank you to *The Herald*'s keen-eyed, quick-witted readers for their ceaseless assistance. It really wouldn't have happened without you.

ONE

Ladies who lurch

AS two male writers, we are always wary about whether we portray women in a proper light in The Diary. But with women becoming more financially independent and going out and enjoying a broader social life than ever before, they can more than hold their own. But just to show that the sexes are still not equal, we recall overhearing a woman from the BBC's Scottish headquarters in Glasgow out for a drink with her pal telling her, 'I have yet to hear a man ask for advice on how to combine marriage with a career.'

A DEBT collector for a catalogue company explained to us the predilection for jewellery among the young women of Glasgow's east end. Starting at Calton, such a woman may wear a single gold necklace and a gold sovereign ring. Further east at Parkhead, a local lady may well have three gold necklaces, gold earrings and four gold rings. Continuing out to Carntyne, a resident is often adorned with five necklaces, one of which will spell her name, and almost all fingers will have some form of gold. 'And when you get to Easterhouse,' he told us in an awed voice, 'it's like Tutankhamun comes to answer the door.'

A COUPLE of Edinburgh office workers popped into a smart George Street brasserie after work the other day to find four very loud, heavily made-up women at the next table who were shrieking and giggling at each other – obviously having been there for some considerable time. As the women eventually got up to leave, one of them stumbled into their table, spilling their drinks, before weaving unsteadily to the door. 'Are they ladies-who-lunch, as the newspapers always put it?' asked one. 'No,' replied his co-worker, 'They are ladies who lurch.'

A GLASGOW mother-of-two phoned her pal in some distress. She and her husband had shared a bottle of wine and got a bit frisky, and she was worried that an unplanned baby was on the way. She was too upset to get a pregnancy kit, so her pal took control and toddled off to the chemist's herself for said kit. While buying it, she realised she was attracting unusual looks from the staff – no doubt associated with the fact that she herself was seven months' pregnant. But rather than throw out the tired old line, 'It's for a friend', she looked them in the eye and sharply declared, 'Look, I'm still not sure. OK?' before waddling out of the shop.

QUEUING up for David Bowie tickets at Glasgow's SECC, Raymond Lowe realised that some of the fans were not as young as they used to be, and perhaps had not been to a concert for a while. This was demonstrated by two female fans who purchased tickets for the standing area and then asked, 'Are they beside each other?'

TWO women of a certain age in Glasgow's West End had taken advantage of some rare good weather to sit on chairs outside the pub to imbibe their Sauvignon Blanc when one opined in a loud voice, 'I've always thought that if you can't be a good example, you can always be a terrible warning.'

THE scene is an upmarket shoe emporium in Glasgow during the sales, when a customer is trying on some very stylish, but not too pricey, footwear, and asks her companion what he thinks. 'Can you actually walk in them?' he enquires, prompting a fellow shopper, dressed to the nines, to interject, 'Walk? Never mind that, dear. At that price, if you can teeter to the gin bottle, buy them.' We are later informed by a female reader that such shoes are known by her friends as 'car to bar' shoes.

TAXI drivers have to gear themselves up for the busiest, but craziest, time of the year at Christmas and New Year as amateur drinkers lose the plot somewhat. One Glasgow driver tells us of a very squiffy young lady being helped into a taxi by a colleague after an office night out. 'Where to?' asked the driver cheerily. 'What the f*** has it got to do with you?' she snarled back.

DRESSING for a family occasion, Paul Cairns's elderly father became concerned by the dubious pattern of a new tie bought for him by Paul's mother. 'Looks like Rangers tartan,' he griped aloud as Mrs Cairns busied herself elsewhere in the house. When Mr Cairns Sr studied the tie's blue tartan hue more closely, his worst fears were confirmed. 'Aye, that's the Rangers tartan,' he asserted angrily. Misinterpreting what she had heard, his wife bustled past him and, staring skywards out of the window, anxiously lamented, 'And the weatherman said it was going to be clear all day.'

A WEST End bar in Glasgow on Saturday afternoon, where two women *d'un certain âge* are meeting for a restorative cocktail after a heavy day's shopping. Suddenly, one of the women starts scrabbling through her shopping bags before announcing a tad too loudly, 'Damn! My doctor said it would help my memory during the menopause if I took Ginkgo biloba – and I've bloody forgotten to buy it.'

TWO women chatting in a Glasgow hairdressers were discussing a recipe in one of the glossy magazines. Eventually, one of them said sagely, 'I read recipes the same way I read science fiction. I get to the end and I think, "Well, that's not going to happen."'

A WOMAN in a Glasgow bar was explaining to the assembled crowd that her sister isn't the brightest and so was asked to give an example. She told them, 'We were playing Trivial Pursuit and she was asked the question, "Which peer disappeared in mysterious circumstances in 1974?" She answered, "Brighton."'

A READER in leafy Lenzie told us that her neighbour recently took her cat to the vet for an operation. All seemed well when she took the cat home. But, later that evening, the phone rang. 'How's your pussy?' the caller asked. Impressed by the caring nature of her vet checking up on the cat at such a late hour, she went into a long diatribe about it still being a bit drowsy after the operation but the stitches didn't seem to be bothering it. Eventually, an exasperated voice on the line interrupted. 'For God's sake! This is a dirty phone call.'

A CHAP told us about his brother-in-law in Currie, Midlothian, who was struggling to squirm under the kitchen sink, which had become blocked. Eventually, he got there and carefully removed the U-bend pipe, neatly catching all the nasty smelly water in a pail. Still lying prone, he eased the full pail out from under the tight spot and asked his watching wife to 'get rid of this'. And, yes, she did indeed pour it down the kitchen sink – only to see it cascade over hubby's upturned face.

THE BBC's magazine *Ariel* normally covers deep issues such as the director general's plans for the future, and what wavebands will be used for new services, so it was good to see a member of staff of BBC Scotland lightening the content the other week. Giving details of her job at Queen Margaret Drive, Glasgow, she then went on to give some insight into her personal life – including the fact that she had a little sun tattooed on one of her buttocks. When the *Ariel* interviewer asked why, she replied, 'So that I can tell people the sun shines out of my arse.'

A RATHER fetching trolley dolly sipping Californian Pinot Noir in a Glasgow West End bar tells us – and who are we to doubt her – of a harassed mother arriving at check-in with a bawling wean in her arms and two other kids either fighting with each other or running away while Mum bellowed at them to come back. The mother was told that due to extra security her suitcases would be searched for firearms and drugs. 'Do you not think that if I had either, I would have used them by now?' the woman snapped back.

WE are assured that a lot of women will know what she meant when we recount that a West End lady, sharing a bottle of Côtes du Rhône with her chums, drained her glass and declared, 'Some days are a total waste of make-up, don't you think?'

WOMEN can be a bit sharp with their own sex. A group in the West End of Glasgow were discussing the kitchen redecoration at the flat of one of their friends, and the fact that another girl, whose decision-making did not impress them, was helping her to choose

the units. 'Oh my god,' said one of them disapprovingly. 'The blonde leading the blonde.'

A FEMALE reader sent us a quiz designed to reveal whether members of the sisterhood are 'Delia Smiths' or 'real women':

- Delia's way: to keep potatoes from budding, place an apple in the bag with the potatoes.
- Real woman's way: buy Smash and keep it in the larder for a year.

- Delia's way: stuff a miniature marshmallow in the bottom of a cone to prevent ice cream dripping through it.
- Real woman's way: just suck the ice cream out of the bottom of the cone, for goodness' sake. You are probably lying on the couch with your feet up eating it anyway.

- Delia's way: when a cake recipe calls for flouring the baking tin, use a bit of the dry cake mix instead and there won't be any white mess on the outside of the cake.
- Real woman's way: Tesco sells cakes. They even do decorated versions.

- Delia's way: cure for headaches – take a lime, cut it in half and rub it on your forehead. The throbbing will go away.
- Real woman's way: take a lime, cut it in half and drop it in a gin and tonic. You might still have the headache, but who cares?

- Delia's way: freeze leftover wine into ice cubes for future use in casseroles and sauces.
- Real woman's way: leftover wine?

TWO

How long is a Glasgow bus?

FRUSTRATIONS at simply travelling around the country whether by car or public transport can lead either to outbreaks of violence . . . or funny stories. Naturally, we prefer folk to contact us rather than punch a fellow traveller's lights out. And thus, we hear of stories such as the reader sitting on the Glasgow suburban train service to Helensburgh who was sitting near a blind chap with his guide dog. At Scotstounhill station, he got up to leave and asked the ticket seller if he could be directed towards the exit out of the station. This perplexed a fellow traveller sitting opposite him, who said to no one in particular once he left, 'Ah thought thae dogs were supposed to know where they were going?'

IAN Guthrie, from Largs, was waiting for a bus at the Royal Alexandra Hospital in Paisley over the festive season, when a chap who joined him at the stop eventually asked him whether, given the lateness of the hour and the time of year, there were any buses due. Ian replied that the timetable on the shelter suggested there was indeed one due, and this being the season of goodwill, he felt the occasion demanded that he make some chatty remark, so he quipped to the stranger, 'Well, if there's no bus within 15 minutes,

you could always steal a car.' Without a pause, the chap replied, 'How did ye know I'm fae Greenock?'

FORMER Beirut hostage Brian Keenan was in Dundee for the Celtic Film and TV Festival, which featured a film about his incarceration. Fortunately, Brian was out of earshot when a young driver sent to collect him – a moonlighting Dundee Uni student – was heard to remark to the hotel porter, 'Do you think he'll dive straight into the car boot?'

SOMETIMES you know a great line but rarely have the chance to use it. However, a Diary reader was very impressed by a demure senior citizen sitting next to him on a flight to Gibraltar who had been moved down from business class because it was overbooked. The lady in question had asked for a complimentary glass of champagne but was curtly told that it was only available in business class. It took a while for the passenger to get her champagne after she explained she would have been in business class if the airline hadn't overbooked. So when the plane almost landed at Gib, but circled round twice because of strong crosswinds before eventually landing with a heavy thump, she was able to smile sweetly at the stewardess and ask with mock seriousness, 'Have we landed – or were we shot down?'

NIALL Macdonald of Bearsden tells us of a plane touching down at Glasgow Airport and breaking unusually sharply because of smoke coming from the port engine. The captain announced that there had been a small fire which had been automatically extinguished, but nevertheless they would have to remain out on the runway until the emergency services arrived. The anxious babble of voices dissolved into laughter when a very Glaswegian voice announced, 'Ah don't mind walkin' it frae here.'

A GREENOCK lawyer wanted to catch the first ferry from Arran, but the service bus driver stopped before the steep hill into Lamlash and said he couldn't risk it as the road was covered in ice. Beside him were three four-by-fours, with drivers taking an equally dim view of going down the road. Eventually, the gritter arrived, but with no grit left. So the lawyer thought her ferry-catching chances were lost until an old Metro car drew up with two chaps in the front and a woman in the back. 'Do you want a lift to the ferry?' the driver asked, and the grateful lawyer jumped in the back as the driver, despite a few slips and skids, made it to the bottom. As she delivered her grateful thanks, the driver told her, 'It's all right. We needed a bit more ballast in the back.' The New Year resolution to visit the gym more is now a top priority, she says.

A BAFFLED English policeman had to deal with a minor traffic accident on the M6 involving a Rangers supporters' bus after a game down south. Fortunately, no one was seriously injured but the supporters had to wait for a replacement coach. The reason the policeman was baffled was that one of the fans had told him, in describing the accident, that, 'I've jist been thrown aboot like a scud book up the back of the class.'

READER George Embleton stopped at Harthill services and was intrigued by a little pudding bowl with a small pile of cash in it near the till. It was also full of water. He considered various reasons why it was waterlogged – a dripping ceiling, perhaps, or a watering dish for anyone travelling with a budgie. So he felt the need to ask the checkout girl. She assured him it was indeed a dish for tips – and the water stopped customers from nicking the coins.

TWO pensioners got on a bus at Knightswood heading to Glasgow Royal Infirmary. 'Two concessions, pal,' said the male of the species holding a few coins in his hand, unaware that one of the wonders of the Scottish Parliament is that pensioners now travel on local bus services for free. 'That's OK,' said the driver, waving them on to the bus. But the chap was not convinced. 'What's the matter? Is the wee box for the money broke?' he asked. 'Naw,' says the driver, 'you can go anywhere for free now.' 'OK,' replied the cheery OAP, 'make it two to Blackpool then.'

IN foul weather, a bus from Glasgow to Cumbernauld broke down in the dark, way short of its destination. The ire of the passengers was not helped by the driver using his mobile phone to tell the depot, 'I've run out of diesel.' Muttering was heard about him not checking the gauge. But he announced that a relief bus would be sent from the

depot. 'How long's it going to be?' asked one angry lady, which gave the driver – who was either brave or stupid – the chance to reply with the classic line: 'I reckon it will be as long as this one.'

WE are told of a group of Glasgow taxi drivers who meet regularly for an early evening meal before they face the rigours of a teeming Saturday-night shift in the city. One of the regulars, a female driver, arrived late, and hurriedly explained, 'I've been lying under a dirty engine for most of the afternoon.' It allowed a fellow driver, who liked to think of himself as a bit of a wit, to innocently enquire: 'Hiawatha?'

CHARLES Provan of Larkhall was in a black cab in Glasgow behind a dear old lady in a near-vintage car. When the lights turned to green she stalled the car, and the queue behind had to wait on another round of lights changing. But when it turned to green again, she again stalled her ageing vehicle. At that, the taxi driver leapt out, walked up to her window and declared: 'Whit's wrang hen, dae nane o' these colours suit you?'

A BUS draws up at a stop in Glasgow. On the back, in that smart, modern, new-technology way, it proudly boasts: 'Find out where this bus goes: www.arriva.co.uk.' Unimpressed, a woman at the head of the queue observes to no one in particular, 'Would it not be easier to run round to the front?'

KEN Henderson, chief engineer of the *Waverley* paddle steamer, raised £1,300 by selling off redundant bits and pieces to enthusiasts, with the money going to the continued preservation of the steamer. Thus, one enthusiast held up a piece of coiled hemp and asked innocently, 'So basically you're looking for money for old rope?'

MORTON chairman Douglas Rae and fellow director Arthur Montford, formerly of *Scotsport* fame, were heading by train for their game against Berwick when they stopped the refreshment trolley and asked the chap what sandwiches he had. 'Well, none actually. No, wait a minute, I do have one, but it's past its sell-by date,' he told them. As they were both diabetic and needed something to top up their insulin, they asked how far past its sell-by date it was. 'Ten minutes,' came the reply. Stunned at such exactitude by ScotRail, they said they could take a gamble with that and buy it anyway. The trolley operator was adamant, however, stating that company policy was that the sandwiches could only be sold for four hours after they were stocked, and it was now four hours ten minutes since the trolley was brought on board. So the sandwich remained unbought. 'Things can only get better,' said a hungry Chairman Rae. They didn't. Morton lost 2–0. 'We'll bring our own piece next time,' he muttered to Arthur afterwards.

MORE ScotRail trolley tales. Reader Alex Ferguson tells us of a friend going through to Edinburgh who asked for two bottles of Smirnoff Ice. After watching the trolleyman set the bottles down on the table then start wheeling his goods away, the customer asked, 'Could you open them?' 'I've no opener,' was the reply. A bemused customer asked how he was expected to drink them only to be told, 'I don't know. I only sell them.'

A READER was sitting in a taxi at traffic lights in Glasgow's West Nile Street when he noticed a queue of people on the pavement alongside. Making conversation, he wondered aloud to the driver what the queue was for. So the driver wound his window down and shouted, 'Whit ur youse queuein' fur?' But the driver was completely ignored. Unruffled, he looked back at his passenger and said, 'Must be for hearing aids.'

ONLY a Glaswegian would take pride in a personalised number plate seen on a four-wheel-drive in the city this week – 2 RAG. And just to emphasise his or her delight in it, the plate had the prefix in small letters 'Once a' and the suffix 'Always a'.

THREE

Wishing on the stars

SCOTS love celebrities – they just don't like showing it too much. And if they can gently take a celeb down a peg or two, they will do so with glee. Many's the time a group of Scots football fans has seen a celeb in a foreign part and urged them over with the cry: 'Can we have a photograph?' As the celeb good-humouredly agrees and saunters over, one of the fans will hand the celeb the camera and pose in front of him with his mates.

FOLK luminaries Josh Macrae and Hamish Imlach were once sent to Glasgow Airport to collect three American legends who were appearing at a folk festival: Ramblin' Jack Elliott, billed as 'America's Roving Cowboy', Blind Gary Davis, the black blues great, and Buffy Sainte-Marie, the Cree Native American. Nervous about the meeting, Josh and Hamish sank a few drinks. Having only seen the visitors on old album covers, Hamish asked Josh, 'How will we recognise them?' Josh replied, 'A blind black man, a Cree Indian and a cowboy? If we don't recognise them, Hamish, I'm giving up drink.'

GLASGOW eatery Bar Budda got all excited, claiming the Dalai Lama and his entourage ate there after speaking to a packed Royal Concert Hall during the Tibetan religious leader's last trip to Britain. This was subsequently denied by the Dalai Lama's staff, but Bar Budda stuck to its story, with a member of staff declaring, 'Our manager says it was him. After all, there's hardly an abundance of orange-anoraked, bald-heided Glaswegians who impart Buddhist wisdoms over dinner.'

RADIO Clyde's Tiger Tim was compèring a Saturday morning children's show when he asked young listeners to phone in and tell him by what name the singer August Darnell was better known. The answer is, of course, Kid Creole, but the listeners were having difficulty with it until one young lad phoned in. Being a bit nervous on radio, he was saying to Tiger, 'Kid . . . Kid . . . Kid . . .' An excited Tiger was encouraging him with a 'Yes, yes, you're nearly there,' until the lad finally blurted out, 'Kid ye repeat the question?'

VISITING London, a reader noted a kerfuffle in a HMV record shop. Yoko Ono was conducting an in-store signing session, autographing copies of the DVD saluting her late husband, John Lennon. She'd been about to inscribe it in the manner requested by its purchaser until her PR man angrily stepped in. It seems the customer had merely been too honest in asking Yoko to append her signature beneath the dedication: 'Dear eBay auction winner'.

EMERGENT band Mydas were keen for their adult guitar-driven indie rock to impress the predominantly teeny-girl audience at the music festival Big in Falkirk, as well as two record-company talent-spotters. Mydas's manager therefore persuaded two thirty-something female chums to initiate the screaming when the band appeared, as well as throw a pair of nicely laundered cream silk pants at their lead singer. The ploy worked, inspiring shrieks and a hail of trainer bras. However, the grown-up pants-thrower was

later forced to ask for them back, sheepishly telling the stage manager, 'They're part of a set.'

SINCE relinquishing his starring role in *Monarch of the Glen*, actor Alastair Mackenzie has grown a full beard. This caused confusion when Alastair, as patron of Dunblane's Queen Victoria School, helped launch its centenary appeal with a display of piping and Highland dance in Edinburgh Castle. Surrounded by adoring fans, Alastair was approached by a crusty old cove with a military air, who brusquely asked, 'And who are you, young chap?' Alastair said he was Alastair Mackenzie, helpfully adding, 'The Laird of Glenbogle.' At this, the elderly gent barked, 'Don't get ideas above your station, laddie – you're one of our bagpipers,' and attempted to frogmarch Alastair back across the room.

JOURNALIST Graham Scott recalled American guitarist Ted Nugent relaxing in what was then the Albany Hotel in Glasgow, following a gig at the Apollo. Ted was sitting in the hotel bar, with a young Glasgow woman on his lap. The woman picked up Ted's Stetson and plonked it on her head as Ted said to her to be careful as it was his lucky hat. 'How come you cry it yer lucky hat?' was the lady's reply, giving Ted the opportunity, of course, to utter the immortal words: 'Just keep wearin' it, honey, you'll find out.'

ACTRESS Zoë Wanamaker has become patron of rural touring company Mull Theatre, which eventually hopes to develop a theatre of its own on the island. Zoë, we recall, was once asked in an interview what her favourite sight was, and she replied, 'The back of my relatives, and the front of my husband.'

SCOTLAND rugby internationalist Kenny Logan ended his trip to the World Cup by staying on in Australia to soak up some sun on Bronte Beach with his TV presenter wife, Gabby. In front of Kenny on the sand was an Asian girl and, after a few minutes, she turned round and asked him if he would mind looking after her bag while she went into the sea. 'What makes you think that you can trust me?' Kenny replied. 'Oh, you have an honest face,' she said. 'Besides,' she continued in a more pragmatic fashion, 'I won't be long . . . I'm just going in to pee.'

AUCHTERMUCHTY'S finest twin exports, Craig and Charlie Reid, otherwise known as The Proclaimers, performed a gig on Bute. Having finished sound-checking by mid-afternoon, Charlie and one of the band's entourage thought they'd pass the time in traditional Scottish seaside manner: by having a shot on the mini-golf. Off they went, quickly encountering a bedraggled, drink-sodden figure weaving unsteadily along Rothesay's promenade. ''Scuse me, are you yon s**** fae the Proclaimers?' the man asked belligerently. 'No,' Charlie replied, 'I'm his brother.'

PAMELA Stephenson, who has written a second book about life with husband Billy Connolly, reveals that when Billy was a young welder sauntering down Renfrew Street in Glasgow with his then 'haywire hairdo', a chap asked Billy, 'Did ye glue yer heid and dive in a barber's midden?' Billy's wife visited Glasgow to promote the book, where she was asked by a *Herald* reader whether it was true that Billy had visited disgraced Tory peer Jeffrey Archer when he was in jail. Pamela confirmed he had, and explained it was because Jeffrey had always been nice to Billy in the past. But Pamela added that Billy's opening line to Jeffrey was: 'Now that you've been shagged by Mexican transvestites on a regular basis, has it changed your political views?'

THE king of Chicago blues, Buddy Guy, was playing at the Usher Hall in Edinburgh when he invited requests from the audience towards the end of the show. At this, a bevvied fan and halfwit shouted out, 'Hey, Buddy. Dae us a favour, dae's a favour, Buddy.' Clearly, he was majoring in incoherence. But all was not lost. The affable Mr Guy said, '"Fever" – I like that song,' and proceeded to do an impromptu but memorable rendition of the Peggy Lee classic.

ACTRESS Susan Hampshire was stopped at an airport she was passing through by a couple who confirmed that it was indeed the *Monarch of the Glen* star, and proceeded to tell her how much they enjoyed the BBC series, and how it was the highlight of their Sunday evening. As Susan made the usual actorly acknowledgements of the couple's praises, they then slightly spoiled the moment by adding, 'Yes, we like nothing better than just turning the sound down and looking at all that lovely scenery.'

TAGGART actor Alex Norton took his family to Norway for a winter holiday as part of the *Scottish Passport* TV series. As he was about to board the plane, a suspicious member of the airline staff spotted he was carrying a banjo. Perhaps because he was a music lover, the crew person said that Alex could not take it on board. So Alex snapped back with the line, 'Why? Do you think I'm going to banjo the pilot?' Fortunately that lost a bit in the translation, and he was allowed to carry on with his journey.

OVERHEARD in Glasgow's east end, according to Gary McMillan: 'J.K. Rowling's an author in Edinburgh? Ah thought jakey-rolling was a sport in Glesca.'

JAZZ legend George Benson, passing through Glasgow Airport after his gig in the city, popped into the Impulse record shop there. After rifling through the album racks, George fixed the shop's young sales assistant with an accusatory glare, stating, 'There's only one of my CDs here.' Nonplussed for a moment, the youth eventually composed a reply which bodes well for his future in retail, insisting, 'That's because we've sold so many.'

GOLFER Gary Player stuttered slightly over a word when he booked into his hotel in St Andrews in preparation for taking part in Sun Microsystems' charity golf marathon. So he cheerily told the hotel staff that he did, indeed, stutter quite badly as a youngster and had sought professional help at a medical establishment that had been recommended to him. Not finding the address he'd been looking for, Gary had asked a chap in the street, 'Excuse me, do you know where the s-s-s-school for s-s-stuttering is?' At that, the passer-by had clapped Gary on the back and told him, 'You've no need to go to school – you can stutter already.'

FOUR

Taking liberties

IT is why, of course, it is called gallows humour. But even when in a court of law, or being interviewed by the polis, there is many a Scot who will turn to a joke when it would have been wiser to have stayed silent. Leading QC Donald Findlay tells of one of his clients being questioned by officers from Strathclyde Police, who asked him, 'Where were you between 7 and 11?' The temptation proved too much for the chap, who replied, 'Primary school. Where were you?'

FORMER police officer Gerry MacKenzie tells us of the time there was a minor crime spree in Glasgow's Saracen district. They knew the miscreant concerned in the break-ins, but unfortunately he was staying well away from his usual haunts. Says Gerry: 'One night, while the troops were in for their piece and listening to Radio Clyde, they heard their prime suspect chatting live with presenter Tiger Tim during a regular phone-in. Tiger's innocent interrogation was faultless, and the arch criminal revealed he was with his pals up in "Spikey's hoose" in Balmore Road having a wee bevvy. They were still chatting when the polis knocked on the door. Half an hour later when the main target was locked up along with his pals on a variety of warrants, they were vowing to track down the poltroon who "grassed them up".'

READER Pat Cassidy of Wishaw was attending the X-ray department at Wishaw General Hospital when a prisoner from Shotts Prison was brought in, handcuffed to two prison officers. As they sat awaiting their turn, they watched a mother being given the runaround by her eight-year-old son who ignored all her demands to behave. As the handcuffed patient was leaving, he nodded at the little tearaway and declared, 'See when ah wis his age, if ah acted like that towards my mother, she'd ave given me a good skelp – and it didnae do me any harm!' before being led away to the prison van.

SHERIFF Albert Sheehan, addressing a reunion of *Falkirk Herald* journalists, told the tale of the woman about to be sentenced by a sheriff who thought a fine would be the best way of disposing with the case. Asking her about her income, the sheriff was told that she had already filled in a form about her background, which was passed up to him. But when he saw under the section on income that the woman had written 'F All', he warned her that the use of such language could be construed as contempt of court and adjourned the case for further consideration. Hearing the case again later, the sheriff listened to the duty solicitor, who rose to explain, 'The accused has only one source of income – family allowance.'

FORMER social-work boss Reg McKay, now a writer, helped Glasgow gangster Paul Ferris pen his opus, *The Ferris Conspiracy*, while Ferris was in Frankland jail near Durham. Reg tells us Ferris had taken an interest in reading in jail and was attempting to work his way through Dostoyevsky's *The Brothers Karamazov*, which he found a bit heavy going. Naturally, though, when a fellow inmate, from the Real IRA, asked what it was, Ferris praised the book to the skies. So impressed was the Irish chap that when he was put in

solitary, he asked to borrow the Dostoyevsky. Two days later, all that could be heard from the chap's cell was a voice shouting, 'Ferris! I'll get you for this when I get out of here!'

A WITNESS in a Port Glasgow case about a street rammy opted for the vernacular when he described how a police car came round the corner – he called it 'a screw motor'. In order to keep the train of thought going, solicitor Alasdair Hendry asked what the people in the street did 'when they saw the screw motor'. 'They bolted,' was the simple reply.

WE are told of a Glasgow supermarket where the security guard gave chase and caught a chap who had failed to pay for the goods stuck in his pocket. As he led the miscreant back into the store to await the police, he noticed the stares of the folk waiting in the queues. So he couldn't resist announcing, 'Nothing to worry about, folks. I just caught him trying to go through the express checkout with 12 items.'

HAVING performed crowd-control duty at an Old Firm game, a Celtic-supporting policeman left Ibrox aboard his official transport home feeling mildly frustrated. He knew he'd have to refrain from celebrating Celtic's victory inside a bus full of his workmates – Rangers fans to a man. He couldn't contain himself, however, on drawing up beside a coach containing jubilant Celtic fans chanting, 'One John Hartson, there's only one John Hartson.' The policeman grinned, surreptitiously punching the air in fraternal salute. At which point, the Celts all began pointing and singing, 'One Fenian polis, there's only one Fenian polis.'

EXECUTIVES at the private firm Reliance Security, which had a raft of poor publicity for losing prisoners when they took over contracts for transporting jailbirds in Scotland, complained to Strathclyde Police about police officers in the custody area at Glasgow Sheriff Court whistling the theme tune to *The Great Escape* when Reliance staff went past. This led to a stern warning from senior police officers to desist. Instead, the inventive cops took to shaking their trouser-legs as a Reliance chap went by – a simulation, of course, of disposing of dug-out earth from the escape tunnels.

EVIDENCE from rural Fife that the police crackdown on driving while using a mobile phone is causing confusion. An Anstruther reader overheard a chap in a pub tell a pal that his phone had gone off that morning while he'd been driving, and he'd swithered for ages wondering whether or not to answer it, before choosing just to let the phone ring. His companion assured him there could be no question that he'd done the right thing. 'Mind you,' said the first chap, 'I was in the middle of a field, driving a tractor.'

VISITING Liverpool from Wishaw, Neil Rowlands had his car broken into and his golf clubs stolen. When police turned up, Neil wondered aloud why the thieves had only taken his clubs and left behind clothing, shoes, food and an expensive squash racket. 'Sir,' replied the young PC in the solemn manner of a Scouse Sherlock Holmes, 'the people who did this are not the sort you'd bump into on a squash court.'

SIX APPEAL

A CONTACT at the courts tells us that two Glasgow QCs began idly chatting before the start of a case. 'Where are you off on your hols?' asked the prosecuting counsel. 'Rhodes,' said his defending opposite number, thereby sparking a £20 bet that defence counsel couldn't work the word 'Rhodes' into his closing speech. And so it came to pass that a malnourished-looking alleged serial housebreaker from Lanarkshire's blasted hinterlands was mildly baffled to find himself, according to his counsel, 'standing before the court today, like the Colossus of Rhodes'.

FIVE

That will teach them

YES, children can be cute, but their observations can also be stunningly accurate. Even in the very young, there can be signs of world-weary cynicism setting in at an early age. In Glasgow's plain-speaking Maryhill, for example, a whirling helicopter above the playground of a nursery caught the attention of a new intake of fresh-faced three year olds. Piping voices were raised in innocent wonder, until one strident voice drowned out the others: 'Ach, it's the polis lookin' for ma da' again.'

A PARTY of seven year olds from a Partick primary school in Glasgow was taken on a trip to Edinburgh Zoo. The penguin enclosure was the focus of great interest, with a pupil staring intently at one of the birds before asking his pal, 'Why's that penguin got a ring round its leg?' Evincing a sagacity beyond his years, the lad's little chum replied, 'It must be a racing penguin.'

BACK to school time. A lady from Larbert was on the early train to Edinburgh a day after the schools went back after summer when her mobile rang. A hapless husband had obviously been left to take his new primary one-er to school on day two, and the moppet was as confused as her father as to which bit of uniform went where. 'Och, put her on the phone. Hullo, darlin' – no, your polo shirt goes on under your pinafore and your sweatshirt goes over your pinafore. Oh! Have you got your vest and pants on first? Let me speak to Daddy – hullo? Yes. Go have a look at the video you took of her yesterday, that should give you some clues.' And thus a crisis is averted and normality restored.

A TEACHER at Glasgow's St Thomas Aquinas is asking her fourth-year class to stay back a few minutes while she hands out their homework for the week ahead. A hand shoots up, and a worried voice pleads, 'Aw, miss, ah've got a sunbed appointment in five minutes.'

A COMMUNITY police sergeant in Glasgow visited a city primary school to give the youngsters the usual warnings about talking to strange men. The talk ended with him handing out rulers to the youngsters with the slogan 'Say No To Strangers'. Within moments, he noticed some of the lads were furiously amending the rulers by trying to erase the 'St' on the final word. It was then he recalled the religious bent of the primary in question.

A PRIMARY teacher in Ayrshire had been helping her class to make Father's Day cards for them to take home. One little six-year-old poppet had carefully written inside her card: 'God. Please make me the same as my dad. Just change one thing. Don't make me fart as much.'

AS the school term stumbled to a close, teachers were being given the occasional box of chocolates or flowers from their little charges. A West Renfrewshire teacher got perhaps the strangest present from an eight-year-old boy – a cucumber. Not even home-grown, but one of Safeway's finest. There was no message attached, or even the faintest suggestion about the state of her love life. So the teacher asked the lad if his mum had said anything

> The Glasgow school attended by Adrian Beers is Bellahouston Academy and not, as we said in his obituary, Bella Houston (page 31, July 16). It is named after an area of the city, not a person.

about the present. He told her, 'Mum says if you slice it very thinly it's good for getting rid of bags under your eyes.'

A TEACHER, and who are we to question such a pillar of society, tells us one of her young charges shouted out, 'Miss, there's a dug in the playground.' Keen to improve his diction she replied: 'I can assure you there is no "dug" in the playground.' Alas, her subtlety was lost on the youngster, who told her, 'Suit yourself, Miss. But it looks a hell of a lot like a dug tae me.'

ONE Ayrshire five year old's second day at school proved especially memorable for her teacher. On day one, the child had an unfortunate accident, necessitating a change of underwear. 'These pants are the school's spare ones,' explained teacher, 'so just remember to ask your mum to wash them so you can bring them back tomorrow.' The next day, as the teacher boarded the bus to work, she espied her charge sitting up the back. 'Mrs Devine!' the child cried eagerly. 'Your knickers are in my daddy's pocket!'

SCARE stories about the health worries surrounding Scottish farmed salmon reminded a reader of the Scottish primary school where, after the news of some oil tanker going aground and leaking its cargo, the teacher asked her P7 class to write about the harmful effects of oil on fish stocks. Eventually, one struggling lad wrote: 'When my mum opened a tin of sardines last night, it was full of oil – and all the sardines were dead.'

READER Michael Boyle and his family moved to France three years ago, with their eight-year-old daughter attending the local village school, where she has become quite fluent in French. Now that the class has begun to learn English, her parents told her, 'Well, you should be good at that. What kind of words are you learning?' 'Words like big and little,' she told them. As her parents joked about how easy that was, she earnestly added, 'Yes, but I don't say big: I've got to say beeg.'

WE are trying to track down the school where the teacher was encouraging her pupils to buy the class photograph by telling them, 'Just think how nice it will be to look at it when you are all grown up and you can say, "There's Jennifer – she's a lawyer," or "That's Michael – he's a doctor."' At that, a small voice piped up from the back: 'And there's the teacher. She's dead.'

IN the interests of inclusivity, the head of a southside Glasgow nursery school told her charges to enact whatever role they wanted in their Nativity play. The morning performance thus featured ten Josephs, eight Marys and seven kings. In the afternoon, it was eight Josephs, four Marys and eleven kings. During this show, a deceptively sage-looking four year old – a full-timer at the school – sidled up to the head, gloomily remarking, 'No' many Marys this efternoon, is there?'

TWO female teachers were in a Glasgow bar at the weekend recovering from their first days back. One of them went to the bar, where a young man told her, 'My mate says he's had you.' She then

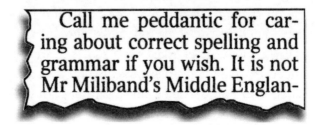

Call me peddantic for caring about correct spelling and grammar if you wish. It is not Mr Miliband's Middle Englan-

excoriated the poor chap in front of everyone for making such an indelicate, and wholly fictitious, claim. It was only when she sat down and explained what happened to her colleague that her friend told her, 'He was only trying to tell you his friend was taught by you.'

A STUDENT teacher is still blushing after his nervous gaffe while taking a class of girls, with an inspector checking up on his work sitting at the back of the class. After the girls had filed in, many favouring the current style of short skirts, the poor chap began his lesson by announcing, 'Right girls, open your legs at page 42.'

SOME three-year-old new arrivals at a Glasgow nursery school were given a talk on an uncharted west of Scotland topic – fruit – with different types being classified according to whether they had pips, seeds or stones. The teacher delivering the mini-lecture felt definite headway was being made, and so chose to risk asking her charges a question. 'What about apricots?' she enquired. 'Has anyone ever had an apricot?' One small boy gloomily stated, 'Yes, but it died.'

READER Mark Johnston recalls his old maths teacher, Bill Russell, telling him of the indignant parent who arrived at the school to tell a teacher, 'How dare you call my wean a f****** doormat.' On closer examination, the teacher realised he had been perhaps a little too demanding in having written on the pupil's report card: 'Faculties dormant.'

READER Kenneth McDonald insists a friend of his was picked on at school in Paisley by bullies who took advantage of his peanut allergy. Asserts Kenneth, 'They were forever taking him behind the bicycle sheds and forcing him to play Russian roulette with a packet of Revels.'

THE stars at Strathclyde University's student freshers' week were the Krankies. The former *Crackerjack!* stars, Ian and his wife Janette, who, of course, dresses up as Jimmy the wee boy, were on stage with a late-night show at the students' union, delighting the young folk with lines like Jimmy scanning the crowd and stating, 'Ah'm looking for ma sister.' 'What's she like?' asks Ian. 'Bacardi Breezers and dope,' says young Jimmy. But the most surreal moment was when Jimmy looked up at Ian and told the audience, 'Do you know he likes his wife to dress up as a schoolboy?'

AN embittered Glasgow school clerkess provided us with an advance copy of her school's handbook for 2004–05, subtly updated for today's parental generation. Its Frequently Asked Questions section opens with:

> Q: Does my child require to attend school between 9 a.m. and 3 p.m.?
> A: No. Just send him/her in when you get up, and if you're still in Braehead Shopping Centre at 3 p.m., don't worry, the staff will look after your child until you return.
> Q: Will I be informed of school events?
> A: You will be sent regular letters/newsletters, but please feel free to throw these in the bin without reading them, then say you never got them.
> Q: Can I buy my child's school photograph?
> A: Yes, but it can be scanned into your computer, then returned, with a note saying you're not happy with it.

SIX

The romantic Scotsman

GLASWEGIANS may no longer pick up a girl at the Plaza dancing, but romance is never far from their thoughts. These days, though, women are more vocal in expressing their disappointment, which is why we overheard one woman in a Glasgow pub telling her pal the gory details of her latest doomed romantic affair. 'He said that ever since he laid eyes on me, he'd wanted to make love to me really badly. So I told him he'd succeeded,' she explained.

A GLASGOW chap turned up at his wife's place of work on a Friday with her passport, intending to whisk her off for a romantic weekend in Paris. So imagine his shock when she told him that she couldn't possibly go at the drop of a hat as she would have to have her hair/nails/fake tan done. Or, as she told her pals, 'I mean, for goodness' sake, there's a time and a place for spontaneity.'

AT a Glasgow snooker hall, a chap had been playing all day with his mates while supping the occasional pint. Normally, a trip to the snooker hall takes an hour, two hours max, but he seemed unable to leave. Later in the evening, the door to the club was thrown open and a woman marched in and emptied a plate of food over his head, before turning on her heel and heading back to the door. The hall had fallen silent and fellow players looked at him expectantly. And with that silly Glasgow bravado, which he is probably still regretting, he had to come up with an answer. 'You forgot the brown sauce,' he shouted.

AN office worker in Dumbarton returned from lunch-time shopping with a fake fur coat and wondered how she was going to tell her husband. 'Just go in wearing it with nothing underneath; he'll never notice the price,' said a colleague. 'I did that once,' said a third staff member. Her workmates were all ears as she explained that one Christmas Eve, as money was a bit tight, she had not bought a present for hubby, but instead lay on the bed wearing nothing but Christmas paper around her body. When hubby returned from the pub she whipped back the duvet to reveal herself in festive splendour. Alas, hubby took one look, declared, 'I don't open my presents till the morning,' and went to sleep.

SADLY, we overheard a chap telling his mate in the pub that he phoned a gorgeous ex-girlfriend to chat about the old days and the passionate time they had. 'I couldn't believe it when she asked if I'd like to meet up. I told her I was a bit older and a bit balder than when she last saw me. But she said it didn't matter. And I told her the stomach was a bit bigger than she would remember. But she just laughed and told me not to be so silly. And she told me that in any case she'd put on a couple of pounds herself. So I hung up.'

WE never tire of good put-downs by barmaids. A chap called Big Tam was in a hotel bar in Hamilton when he heard a bespectacled, well-oiled customer tell one of the barstaff, 'You're very attractive, did you know that? I love your smile and you've got a very attractive walk. In fact, you're lovely.' She barely paused before telling him, 'See if I was wearing your specs, do you think I'd find you attractive?'

WE overheard a young philosopher in a Glasgow pub as she consoled her friend after yet another affair of the heart went sour. 'The thing you've got to remember,' she told her pal, 'is that everyone seems normal until you get to know them.'

SHORTLY before its annual round of first communions, a Roman Catholic church in Glasgow's east end summoned the intending communicants' adult sponsors – mainly aunts and uncles – for a pep talk. The priest reminded them of their task's serious life-long implications, and asked them to draw upon the same qualities they themselves would expect from a partner in marriage. 'You'd be looking for someone considerate, kind, reliable, honest, trustworthy,' he said. At this, one of the aunts present finished swigging her can of Irn-Bru and added, 'And good in bed.'

WE fear terrible chat-up lines at the Christmas party season. A chap in Yates's Wine Lodge in Glasgow told a young woman, 'Ah've got the body of a god.' Fortunately, she was able to give the perfect reply. 'Whit, Buddha?'

A CHAP in Glasgow thought he would impress his girlfriend by taking her for a gourmet dinner at Loch Lomond's Cameron House Hotel where the pots and pans were being rattled by legendary chef

Albert Roux, founder of the Michelin three-star Le Gavroche in London. Sadly, his partner was not impressed, stating that she had never heard of Albert Roux. When the boyfriend insisted that he was indeed world famous, she came back with the sure-fire argument, 'Well, how come I've never seen him on *Ready Steady Cook*?'

TWO young women attending the launch party of the Glasgow Art Fair in George Square met in the scrum for the free booze. 'I'm here to search for some Old Masters,' one of them trilled over the noisy throng, then added, 'Basically, any man over 21, wearing black horn-rimmed specs and a leather jacket.'

BLIND dates. Always fraught occasions apparently. We hear of a Glasgow chap out on such an occasion who had taken the well-worn precaution of getting a pal to phone him after half-an-hour to give him an excuse to leave, if required. As the conversation with the lady concerned had been slower than a snail in treacle, he answered his phone, put on a serious look, and told the lady that he had to go as his father had taken unwell. His date for the evening, not being a complete idiot, snapped back: 'Listen, another ten minutes and my father would have been ill as well, you know.'

WE hear of a woman whose husband never did any housework, declaring it was women's work, even though they both had full-time jobs. So she was astonished to come home one night to find the house hoovered, the ironing done and a cooked meal waiting for her on the table. Standing there was her husband, who told her, 'I read a magazine article which said wives would be more romantically inclined if they weren't so tired from working and running a household at the same time.' When she told her friends the next day, they eagerly asked, 'How did it work out?' 'Well, the dinner was great – but then he said he was too knackered for the romance,' she told them.

AH, the romantic Scotsman. It seems that after fire badly damaged the plush Dunblane Hydro, a number of husbands told their wives that they had been planning a secret weekend of St Valentine's wining and dining at the hotel which had to be cancelled because of the fire. We know this because two such wives telephoned the hotel to find out when it is going to be fully functional. And both were told that the hotel had no record of their husbands ever making such a booking.

CYNTHIA Forrest, a member of the Mearns and Whitecraigs Flower Club on the douce southside of Glasgow, tells us of the five rules for women which a member was circulating among fellow members this week in between the flower arranging:

- It's important to have a man who helps you around the house and has a job.
- It's important to have a man who makes you laugh.
- It's important to have a man on whom you can count and who doesn't lie to you.
- It's important to have a man who loves you and spoils you.
- It's important that these four men don't know each other.

SEVEN

Smiling in the rain

HOLIDAYS can be baffling times as cultures clash and misunderstandings abound. A reader who'd returned from Egypt sent us a story that the lift attendant in his hotel had told him. A female German tourist had entered the attendant's lift, and in a friendly fashion, he'd asked the tourist her name, only to hear the response, 'It's secret.' Rather bemused, he saw her the next day and again asked her, and again was told, 'It's secret.' This happened the following day, which again baffled him. So when she checked out, he could stand it no longer and asked the receptionist the name of the woman who had just left. 'Sigrid,' he was told.

PASSING through Biarritz airport, a reader overheard a well-to-do couple travelling with a frail, elderly woman in a wheelchair who was evidently hard of hearing. 'We've just told everyone here you're 80,' shouted the younger woman apologetically, 'because we can't remember the French for 79.'

THERE is the story about the family packed in their car with suitcases on the roof rack. A neighbour cheerily sees them leaving and inevitably asks, 'Off on your holidays?' When the driver

confirms that they are, she guesses, 'Corfu?' 'Naw,' he tells her, 'we've still to pick up the mother-in-law.'

AN Irish émigré recently went home for the weekend, choosing to enjoy a sunny afternoon drive to the coastal town of Carlingford. She was pleasantly surprised to find the place was buzzing. Keen to discover Carlingford's full range of activities, she popped into its tourist information centre, run by a grey-haired female volunteer. When the visitor said she hadn't realised Carlingford had so much going for it, the old woman replied in all seriousness, 'Aye, we like to keep it quiet.'

DURING the winter, reader Marlene Barrie stopped at a pub in Tyndrum and ordered a whisky and soda with ice. On being told there was no ice, Marlene agreed to have it without. Lo and behold, though, when the drink arrived, it contained a large quantity of ice, albeit oddly shaped. Later, Marlene visited the pub's toilets, located in an outhouse. She couldn't help noticing a row of icicles hanging from the cistern – especially as there was a gap where two had obviously just been removed.

SCOTS businessman Alex Barr had flown to Biarritz with the family on holiday when, on passing through the terminal, he noticed a chap holding up a sign for Serge Blanco. Now Serge was, of course, a rugby legend for France, tormenting Scotland on numerous occasions before retiring, so Alex prevailed on the family to delay the holiday for a few minutes while he celebrity-spotted Serge being met from a flight. So, after hanging around for quarter of an hour to indulge Dad, the Barr family saw a chap, clearly a lot older than France's most-capped player, strolling up to the fellow holding the card for Serge Blanco and walking out of the terminal with him. Disappointed at his mistake, Alex walked outside telling his family what were the chances of there being two Serge Blancos – and in front of them was the Serge Blanco Car Hire Company, which the two chaps were walking into.

WE hear of a couple who finally managed to have their first barbecue of the year and invited the neighbours round. As the lady of the house remarked how good the weather was, hubby joined in with the information that it was forecast to rain the next day. 'Och, you always say it's gonnae rain the 'morra. There's a name for people like you, who always think it's gonnae rain.' 'Aye,' pipes up a neighbour. 'Scottish.'

CAN we believe the member of the Tartan Army planning a trip to see Scotland play in the Faeroe Islands who was astounded when his wife expressed a desire to go with him? As this was not what he expected, he tried to talk her out of it by saying the Faeroes would be cold at that time of year and there would be little there to interest her. 'Cold in Egypt? You must be joking,' his wife replied.

WE overheard a girl in a West End hostelry telling her pals that she and her hubby were going to Dublin for the weekend and that she had told him they would be spending more time in the hotel bedroom than normal. 'The poor soul,' she explained, 'is going around with a big grin on his face. He doesn't realise that it's about the only place left in Dublin where I can have a fag.' And speaking of the cigarette ban in Irish pubs, bar-room philosopher Des

McEntee of the Press Bar cheekily wonders, 'So, all these so-called Irish bars in Glasgow that boast about their authenticity. Are they going to ban smoking as well?'

A VISITOR to the north of Scotland from Glasgow saw at first hand the difficulties some publicans have in introducing a partial smoking ban. In one comfortable bar, the owner had put a sign up stating that smoking would no longer be tolerated in the lounge bar as food was also being served there, but smoking would continue in the public bar. This proved unpopular with one regular who had constantly to be told to put his cigarette out as he preferred being in the lounge to the bar. Muttering away into his pint, the thwarted smoker spotted one customer further up the lounge whose dog was padding around behind him. 'Here!' he shouted at the owner. 'How come I cannae smoke in here, but that dog can run wild?' At that, the owner delivered his Solomon-like wisdom: 'It's no smoking, is it?'

A YOUNG suntanned girl is in Glasgow Airport's departure lounge, heading to London on easyJet when she unknowingly entertains her fellow travellers by having a furious shouting match with her mother over her mobile phone. But, as she reaches the

security area, the uniformed chap gestures to her that her mobile telephone has to go through the scanner. Not giving up, though, she barks, 'Wait! Wait!' down the phone to her poor mum, waits impatiently for it to go through the machine, snatches it up, and continues shouting at her.

AN Edinburgh reader tells us of being in Durham Cathedral where a supercilious guide was explaining every stone and pane of glass to his group of visitors in a haughty manner. Eventually, they reached the stained-glass window of the Last Supper, where the guide tells people to look for the bread, and then for the wine, and then for the fish. 'But,' continues the triumphant guide, 'there is no mention of fish in the story of the Last Supper.' At that, a quiet Glasgow voice piped up. 'Maybe,' said the fed-up tourist, 'it is a depiction of the last fish supper.'

SHOULD we be worried about Beecraigs Country Park in the Lothians, which has listed a number of outdoor activities on its website? Among the attractions, it lists: 'Archery – Targeting Pensioners'.

THREE boyhood Glasgow chums undertook a French Alpine cycling holiday. One owns a confectionery factory. Another is a postman. The third is a roofing contractor. Drinking in their pension late one night, the trio fell into polite conversation with the landlady. In halting Franglais, she enquired about their jobs *en Écosse*. The sweetie-maker successfully mimed his occupation. Ditto the postman. The roofer, however, was far drunker than his compatriots, as well as more unshaven and dishevelled. Struggling to keep his eyes in focus, he brought his two sets of fingertips together at 90 degrees, forming the apex of a roof. '*Mais, oui,*' the landlady said, studying the dissolute, swaying figure before her knowledgeably. 'E eez a priest.'

GLASGOW's city treasurer, Craig Roberton, on a trip to Prague, entered a public loo where the custom is to make a voluntary cash contribution. The city treasurer offered the attendant some coinage only to be met with a torrent of local language. Had he not paid enough for the comfort break? Not understanding a word of it, the good councillor pressed on with his mission, but glancing back for a second, all became clear. In halting English, the attendant held up some toilet tissue, posing the question, 'Do you need a sheet?' 'No,' the city treasurer responded. 'I'm only in for a pee.'

EIGHT

It's a sair fecht

ENGAGING in childhood reminiscence, a group of 40-something Glaswegians listed the strange utterances of their auld Scots grannies. One remembered being puzzled by his gran's habitual reflection 'It's a sair fecht'. Another cited 'Away and pap peas at yer granda'. Others recalled 'Yer heid's fullae wee motors', and 'It's san-ferry-ann tae me'. The mood of cosy nostalgia was undermined when another chum recollected his sweet old granny, evidently from one of Glasgow's more plain-speaking areas, prefacing most meal-times with 'If it disnae stick in yer throat, it'll no' stick in yer arse – so eat it'.

PAINTER and author Alasdair Gray was finishing off his eight-month labour of love – the fantastical ceiling painting of stars, zodiacal imagery and phases of the moon in the OranMor music centre and meeting place at the former church at the top of Byres Road. Alasdair, who, like Michelangelo, had to lie on his back on scaffolding for some of the intricate painting, was working away one day when a workie stopped below him, gaped at the ceiling, and bellowed, 'That's absolutely crackin' up there!' Alas, Alasdair failed to realise it was a compliment, jumped to his feet and

PITY THE POOR DYSLEXIC STONEMASON!

feverishly shouted, 'Oh my God, where's it cracking?' before onlookers calmed him down.

A SENIOR official at Glasgow City Council was remembering one of Her Majesty the Queen's visits to the west of Scotland. Met by the then Lord Provost and his couthy wife, Her Majesty was being shown around various worthy establishments when the schedule left her with a minute or two to chat with the LP and the city's first lady, who, of course, was wearing a new outfit for the occasion. It was then the first lady showed all her Glasgow charm by telling the Queen, 'You know Your Majesty, I bet you're just like me and can't wait to get those shoes off because they're killing you.' The Queen puzzled over this for a moment before replying crisply, 'Quite.'

TONY Blair's former press secretary Alastair Campbell says one of his most embarrassing moments was being on a barge on the Thames standing next to the Duke of Edinburgh. Trying to think of something to say, Campbell blurted out to the Duke, 'Do you think you'd be able to steer one of these?' The Duke fixed him with a baleful look and barked, 'I was a bloody naval commander.' Campbell took that as a yes, then.

TELEVISION news programme *Scotland Today* celebrated its 30th birthday, but a documentary about the show did not include the time a reporter was perplexed to be sent to Edinburgh to cover a member of the Royal Family opening a branch of Berni Inns. He queried the veracity of such an unlikely event with his no-nonsense

51

news editor, only to be brusquely told not to be so smart and just get on with it. When the reporter arrived at the specified address, he discovered that a royal was indeed there – but he was actually unveiling an exhibition of Renaissance sculpture by Bernini.

GLASGOW minister Paul McKeown tells us: 'I was taking a walk while on holiday at Crieff Hydro when I spotted an ornamental fountain with some words of Jesus engraved on it. The text was John 4:13–14: "Whosoever drinketh of this water shall thirst again. But whosoever drinketh of the water that I shall give him shall never thirst." It kind of took the shine off the message a wee bit when I spotted a modern sign beside the fountain saying, "This water is not suitable for human consumption."'

AH, the charm of our traffic wardens. A driver in Glasgow seeing his car outside his house about to be ticketed went out to remonstrate with the chap in greeny-blue, using the argument that it was a Bank Holiday. Without looking up from his book, the warden replied, 'It's no' a Bank Holiday for me, pal' and kept on writing.

THE fire which badly damaged Glasgow's famous gay club Bennets prompted a reader to ask us: 'Is there any truth in reports that the fire was so large that it was attended by 100 firefighters, assisted by 24 red Indians, 16 NYPD officers and 34 building site workers?'

WRITER Fiona Cowan, now living in the East Midlands, anticipated Radio Clyde's 30th reunion party by reminiscing about her days there as a purchase ledger clerk. 'I was once manning the reception desk when a notorious middle-aged Lothario crept up behind me, through the mailroom door, and purred in my ear, "What would you say to a little bonk?" Thank heaven for adrenalin in a tight corner. I smiled up at him and said, "Hello, little bonk." He didn't seem to think that was funny.'

AN émigré reader, resident in Sussex, proffered this editorial correction from his local newspaper: 'Due to a mis-hearing on the phone, we reported last week that the newly-weds, Mr and Mrs Craig, would be living in Hastings with the bride's father. They will in fact be living at the Old Manse.'

TWO chaps in a white van in Partick were reading in their favourite newspapers about the Beckhams coping with allegations about David's close friendship with his former personal assistant when one appeared puzzled and asked his mate, 'What do you think Posh meant when she said she'd been through a lot worse than this?' His mate thought long and hard before replying, 'Did you ever see her movie *Spice World*?'

A POPULAR place at Easter is Palacerigg Country Park in Cumbernauld, where the staff trot out as many newborn lambs, chicks, ducklings and calves as possible to make the visitors feel all soft and cuddly. Scott McMillan, who works there, was down beside the lambs which have to be bottle-fed. They are supplied by a local farmer who has already sprayed them with his identity

mark, BN. As the lambs chomped furiously on the bottles, a woman visitor was heard to cluck sympathetically, sigh, and tell her children, 'They graffiti everything nowadays.'

READER Alistair Wilson observed a frank early-morning exchange in the car park outside the Esporta fitness centre near his home in Milngavie. A bulky bodybuilder chap approached a car parked in a disabled bay and asked the driver, 'Are you disabled?' When the rule-flouting driver replied, 'No,' the bodybuilder enquired, 'Would you like to be?'

SOME Glasgow guys have not been around very much. One chap eventually took the plunge and bought his girlfriend a bunch of flowers for the first time, and he watched as she excitedly put them in a vase of water. Calling back round a few days later he looked at the flowers, the vase now only half full of liquid, and asked, 'Why did you take some of the water out?'

A BUFFET supper was being held at Clydebank Boilermakers Club, where the guests shuffling along the buffet table with their plates were met by a steward holding a tray of polystyrene cups. Expecting the usual query of 'red or white?' a guest was taken aback when the server asked, 'Cheese or coleslaw?' Thinking she had misheard, she asked him to repeat the question. 'Cheese or coleslaw?' he said, and as she still looked blank he added, 'Fur yer baked potato.'

NINE

A pint of Barnardo's

THE traditional Scottish pub has been fighting off attacks from all sides – whether it be the growth in theme bars which discourage the old, the hectic pace of work which discourages colleagues going for a drink, or the health fanatics who simply discourage drink. But there are still examples of the worn-linoleum bar where cheery insults are traded across the counter. We well remember the old tale of the chap going into the pub which advertised in its window 'A pie, a pint and a kind word'. After having a pint of slops slammed down in front of him and a greasy pie shoved across to him by a sullen-faced barmaid, he shouted back to her, 'Hey, what about the kind word?' She thought for a moment, pointed at the plate, and said, 'Don't eat the pie.'

NEWS that the ban on smoking in New York bars means that even ashtrays are *verboten* – in case they encourage people to smoke – reminded one Glasgow chap of a visit, some time ago, to Bishopbriggs bar and landmark, Quin's. He recalled nipping in there once for a libation and flicking his fag ash into the pristine ashtray on the bar only for the barman to whip it away and bawl, 'Hey! Use the flair like everyone else.'

GLASGOW comedian Janey Godley ran a bar in Glasgow's Calton for 15 years. She told us: 'When I had the bar I refused to serve this scarred drunk man whose face looked like a map of the M1. He said, "Do you want a sore face?" I laughed and told him, "Why? Are you giving that one away?"'

READER Gary Stewart was dining in a well-known Glasgow restaurant where he had a giant langoustine as a starter. After dispatching most of it, he embarked on the more difficult task of extracting the remaining meat from the claws, but felt he needed a more specialist tool to help him. 'Excuse me, do you have any crackers?' he asked the waitress. 'No, sir,' she replied, 'but we do have oatcakes.'

ALAN Mitchell noticed that in a pub in Johnstone, the well-intentioned people at the Scottish health education unit had displayed a poster in the gents warning: 'Don't let too much drink spoil a good night out.' This had obviously attracted the brain cells of one of the customers who, after a few moments of wrestling with the concept, had added below it: 'Too much drink IS a good night out.'

A GROUP of friends congregated in a somewhat pretentious bistro bar in Edinburgh. When the group's third or fourth round of drinks was delivered, the waitress asked the man doing the honours how he would like to pay. She was less than amused when he replied, 'Same way as always in here – through the nose.'

RETURNING home to Fife after having trotted the globe, Nazareth's bassist Pete Agnew was in his local in Dunfermline when a chap came in and asked what the soup of the day was. Jim the barman told him it was lentil. A frown creased the customer's face and he stated, 'Aw, c'moan, it's been lentil the last three months.' The barman thought upon this before delivering a pearl of Solomon-like wisdom: 'Aye, well . . . there's no' much ye can dae wi' lentils.'

WE are told of the licensed premises which only does cooked food at lunch-time on its busy days towards the end of the week. Earlier in the week, it does filled rolls instead. And, of course, on the days of hot food, it is only available until two o'clock. Thus, on a Friday, a couple of strangers walk in at three in the afternoon and ask if they do filled rolls. 'We dinnae dae filled rolls when the kitchen's open,' they were told. 'Oh, the kitchen's open,' they say, excitedly. 'Can we have a meal then?' 'Sorry, kitchen's shut.' We believe this is what philosophers call a logical contradiction, although that would be of little sustenance to the hungry but bemused customers.

THE Eagle pub in Prestwick, where two chaps are seen approaching the *Who Wants To Be a Millionaire?* quiz machine. One says to the other, 'You hit the screen and I'll stand behind you and cough.'

IT could easily happen. An American tourist telling everyone in the bar in Millport how much he loves Scottish beer points at the beer tap and asks loudly for a pint of Barnardo's. The puzzled barman eventually explained to the chap that it was in fact a charity can draped over the front of the font.

READER Bill Brown of Cardonald, Glasgow, was in licensed premises in Aberdeen where an awful DJ was failing to get anyone on the dance floor. In exasperation, the disc jockey asked the bored crowd, 'Is there anythin' ye want me tae pit oan fur youse?' It was inevitable, of course, that someone shouted back, 'Aye, yir jaiket.'

SIMILARLY, Dr Bill Thomson in Bothwell recalls an office function where a miserable four-piece band was getting little response. The band leader asked if there was anything the crowd would like them to play. 'Dominoes,' came the reply.

SOMEONE not quite clear on the concept of peppermint tea was a waitress in a south side of Glasgow eaterie who was asked for one. Sure enough, the pot arrived at the table smelling strongly of mint. The only snag was the brown liquid which came out of the pot. The woman who ordered the tea looked inside and discovered a bog-standard Typhoo tea bag and a large mint leaf. When she remonstrated with the waitress she was told, 'Well, we ran out of peppermint tea bags, and this is the best we could do.'

A GROUP of Scots lawyers was visiting Royal Wimbledon Golf Club where one of the chaps, feeling a bit delicate after a few libations with his dinner the night before, asked the barman for two Cokes in a pint glass with ice. The barman, clearly struggling with the refined yet Scottish accent, asked for the order to be repeated. It was, and three minutes later he appeared at the chap's table with two wine corks in a pint glass resting on some ice cubes.

BEST excuse for going home early from the pub. A chap in Glasgow was being pressured by his drinking buddies to stay for just another pint. But he managed to extricate himself with the declaration, 'I'm sorry, lads. I need to get home early – the wife's got laryngitis, and I don't want to miss it.'

IAIN Fenton tells us of his local, where food is served between 12 and 2. A couple of hillwalkers arrived at 11.30 to be told that the kitchen wouldn't open till 12 so they decided to have a drink and wait. Now, this is a Scottish pub where the clock is set a quarter of an hour fast in order to aid staff at drinking-up time, but of course the hillwalkers didn't know this. And so, when the hands of the clock hit 12, the walkers went back to the bar asking for food, only for the manager to bark, 'I telt ye the kitchen disnae open till 12,' sending the puzzled couple back to their seats. 'Service like that you just can't buy,' says Iain.

NEIL Dunlop tells us of his wife and friends visiting an inn on Arran where, after much deliberation, someone ordered a sambuca liqueur. When the sambuca arrived, the person who ordered it wanted to go the whole hog and have a coffee bean put in it, and have it briefly set alight, in order to add to the drink's flavour. So the barmaid was asked for a coffee bean for the sambuca. After a few minutes searching, she returned to state that the search had been fruitless – but would a spoonful of Nescafé do instead?

A CHAP in a Glasgow bar had obviously practised his lines the other night when he told a work colleague, 'I met my wife at a singles night.' 'Really?' replied his colleague, which allowed him the follow-up line, 'Yes, and I thought she was at home looking after the kids.'

TRENDY Glasgow bar Tiger Tiger installed strips of sandpaper along the top of the toilet-paper holders in the cubicles to stop wilder elements using the surfaces to snort illegal powders. One innocent checking out the toilets remarked, 'A strip to file your nails on? That's fantastic.'

DREW Moyes of Ayr tells us that a stranger, as happens in the summer, had wandered into a local boozer where a customer, to be welcoming, asked if he was on holiday. The chap said that he was indeed, so the local pressed on, asking him where he was from, to be told York. Emboldened by the chat, the visitor returned the courtesy and asked the local where he was from. 'Me? I'm frae here in Ayr,' the local replied. And after thinking about this for a few moments, the visitor asked him, 'Oh, you mean you're a sort of vagrant?'

PUB-GOERS have a tendency to stick with a name even if a pub has changed hands. Thus, Gordon Chalmers tells us about the Empire Bar in Bannockburn which changed hands in the late '60s and was renamed The Jolly Beggars. The new owner was beside himself that no one would ever refer to the place as anything other than the Empire, but was no doubt heartened that after he sold up and left, the place was rechristened as the Empire, and became known thereafter as The Jolly Beggars.

THE son of Scottish footballing legend Jim Baxter, Stephen, has followed his late dad into the pub trade, and has taken over the Old Toll Bar on Paisley Road West, Glasgow, which sits on a corner site and has three entrances. Just before it closed for renovations, he had to tell a drunk who staggered in that he would not be served. The chap departed grumbling, only then to re-enter through the next door. Again, his custom was declined. And, yes, he did actually come through the third door, and when Stephen patiently explained for the third time that he wouldn't be given a drink, the irked customer shouted, 'Do you own every pub in this road?'

TWO fine chentlemen from Skye returned from their first visit to America and told friends of their arrival at their Florida resort late on a Friday evening, when they decided they needed a wee libation. They popped into the local bar and after a few drams, one of the bar staff vigorously started to ring a bell. Dan looked at his watch and as it was around 10.45 p.m. he said, 'Here, it's last orders, you'll have a double?' After a couple of large ones were set up at 11 o'clock, another member of staff rang the bell, so, tired and weary, they swallowed up and headed off to bed. The next night in the same bar they asked when last orders would be. 'The usual time,' they were told, '2 a.m.' Puzzled, one of the Skye men asked, 'Strange licensing laws to close at 11 on a Friday night but at two in the morning on the Saturday going into the sabbath?' And, yes, it was then patiently explained to them that they closed at two every night – but the bell was rung every time someone gave the staff a hefty tip.

TEN

Rice or chips?

A SENIOR Taiwanese businessman, chairman of a large semiconductor company, was addressing portfolio managers in New York when the question of droughts in Taiwan was brought up. He explained it was an issue of priorities for the Taiwanese government, which had to decide whether scarce water resources should be made available for the rice farmers' paddy fields or the semiconductor manufacturers. It was too much for a Glasgow expat who found few of the New Yorkers understood him when he blurted out, 'Rice or chips – I've been asked that question many times.'

FIFE PE principal Willie Allan tells us he was in the company of a retired Fife miner who was being pestered by a chap who had a fascination for what it must have been like to be a miner. Eventually, when the chap asked, 'What kind of lamps did you use?' the old miner told him, 'I don't know. I was constantly on day shift.' Willie also insists there is a housing scheme in Fife with so many windows boarded up, the local window cleaner carries a sander.

WE often employ the word 'apocryphal' to excuse our use of old and/or dubious yarns. We only mention it because reader Ross Miller tells us of an electrician and apprentice at ScottishPower installing a heating system in an old dear's home in Paisley. As the tradesman was lodged head-first in a cupboard, the old lady's terrier ran at him full tilt and lodged its teeth into his thigh. The agitated home-owner rushed through to see the terrier hanging on with its teeth and the apprentice pulling at its hind legs. So she shouted at the apprentice, 'Kick its balls, son.' With one swift swing of his sizeable workboot, the apprentice duly did, sending the yapping mutt into orbit. At that, the mortified dog-owner screamed, 'Naw, son, naw. His tennis balls.' And they never did get the customary tea and biscuits.

TWO recent graduates were having a pint in Curlers in the West End of Glasgow, discussing job interviews. One of them told his mate that he'd been offered a job which paid £4.20 an hour, but the employer said that in six months' time, all being well, it would go up to £5. 'What did you say?' asked his pal. 'I said I could start in six months,' his mate replied.

THE scene is Dunblane High Street where the rain is teeming down and the wind is blowing. A passer-by sees a street-cleaner going about his duties and greets him with a cheery, 'It's a rotten day for that job.' The sweeper, obviously a bit of a philosopher, dryly replies, 'Every day's a rotten day in this f****** joab.'

APPLICATION forms? Tom Kelly of Linlithgow recalls a form his wife received when she was a manager at Littlewoods. Under 'First language' the applicant had written: 'Said "Dada" at six months'. Similarly, Margaret McCulloch's husband insists he was once asked to scrutinise an application form which had posed the question: 'Do you have a police record?' The hopeful job-seeker had replied: 'Yes – "Don't Stand So Close to Me".'

A CHAP in a mortgage-broker's firm in Perthshire tells us that a colleague went out to a potential client's house and was a bit worried to see their scrawny dog prowling the garden when he opened the gate. When the couple opened the door, though, and he went in to discuss their mortgage needs, the dog seemed reasonably docile as it followed them into the house. The appointment was going rather well until the dog roused itself and peed against one of the chairs. The mortgage chap was mortified and didn't know what to say. However, the couple said nothing either, leading to a prolonged period of silence. The meeting seemed to end quite quickly after that, with the chap not knowing if he had completed a deal. A few days later, his angry boss summoned him into his office to explain himself after the couple sent a letter of complaint about the chap bringing his un-housetrained dog with him when he made the house call.

STAFF in a Glasgow city-centre office were naturally supportive when a fellow worker, named Tom, revealed he was lactose intolerant. Ever since, they've called him Tom Soya.

AN East Kilbride reader assures us an unemployed pal was once forced by dole office mandarins to apply for a job in which he was not remotely interested. The application form featured the question: 'Have you been in the Army?' The reluctant job-seeker entered an affirmative reply. The next question asked: 'What was the reason for your discharge?' He duly wrote: 'A burd I met at the Locarno.'

THE scene is a Lanarkshire office where the boss is giving his annual appraisal to the office junior. The bulk of it is good but his one slight criticism is that the junior is not using his initiative often enough. 'But you never told me to,' came the swift reply.

A BURGER van at Jordanhill station in Glasgow's West End is surrounded by a crowd of lads from no-nonsense St Thomas Aquinas Secondary when a uniformed girl from the rather more upmarket Jordanhill School arrives and asks for a roll and potato scone, also requesting could she have 'the scone fried crisp at the

edges and soft in the middle'. The burger-flipper ponders briefly, wondering whether his alfresco mobile establishment has been mistaken for the conservatory of the neighbouring Three Sisters restaurant. He then replies, 'Look, hen, you can have it burnt, like everybody else's.'

A GLASGOW businessman confesses that he was attending a company do at a smart London hotel when he had perhaps just a little too much to drink. He awoke during the night requiring the loo, but in his still-fuzzy state he opened the wrong door and staggered out into the hotel corridor before realising what he had done. Of course, the room door locked behind him and, to make matters worse, he sleeps in the nude. Eventually, he could think of no other plan but to take the lift down to the lobby, praying fervently there would be no one around as it was three in the morning. On leaving the lift to approach the night porter, he espied a newspaper discarded on a chair, which he thankfully picked up to cover his embarrassment. Thus approaching the desk with newspaper to the fore, he explained what happened, asked for a spare room key, and said, 'Well, at least I've not totally embarrassed myself by having to stand here completely naked.' 'That would, indeed, be correct, sir,' said the haughty porter, 'if it were not for the security camera in the lift.'

BARELY seven days after building a brick wall outside a Glasgow school, two seasoned council workmen resignedly set about the inevitable task of removing it again. Striving to affect the right air of proletarian affability, the school's upper-crust heidie quizzed the duo as to the whereabouts of their hod. 'A hod?' riposted the workmen with a note of scorn. 'Hods is things o' the past, missus. It's the young guys noo – they huvny the shou'ders furra hod. In fact, missus, young guys noo huvny goat the shou'ders furra pair o' braces.'

RICE OR CHIPS?

SPEAKING with brisk clarity over the phone, a Glasgow businesswoman advised a client in London to direct his enquiries elsewhere within the company. 'Write to my colleague Alex Taylor,' she said. The next day, her office received a letter which caused widespread consternation. It bore the address: 'Macaulay Garlic Taylor.'

A LARGE office in East Kilbride, where a chap called George is wary of letting the young work-experience person do too much unsupervised. But eventually a call of nature takes George from his desk where he leaves the youngster to answer his phone. Which is why the rest of the office was smirking when the lad picked up the phone and intoned, 'George? No, he's gone to the toilet. But he'll be back in two shakes.'

ELEVEN

Moses in Edinburgh

AS Scotland depends increasingly on tourism to earn a dollar or two, our politicians would like to think there is always a warm welcome for visitors no matter where they arrive in Scotland. Our research would appear to show, though, that pawky Scots humour can still filter past the plastic smiles. A guide on a Loch Ness monster-watching tour confessed to us that he had his fill of a woman from South Africa on his tour during the winter, who complained about the weather and even about the non-visibility of the monster. So when she angrily asked him, 'Why do they put salt on the road? It's marking my shoes,' he could not stop himself from replying, 'It makes the road taste better when you slip on it and fall on your face.'

SINGER Roy Gullane was taking the train to Oban from Glasgow when a German tourist looking out of the window asked what the expanse of water was that they were passing. A local chap who had been swigging from a carry-out on his table came to the rescue and announced, 'That's Loch Awe.' 'Really?' said the tourist, who then pointed out the window on the other side of the train and asked what they were passing there. The

tourist was ever so puzzled when his helpful travelling companion told him, 'Och, that's f*** a'.'

AN RAF helicopter was called in when an elderly Austrian couple found the going a bit tough on Ben Nevis, and other walkers phoned the police to say they needed assistance. The RAF crew was taken aback though when it winched them aboard and the elderly chap's wife proffered a gold credit card to pay for the chopper. She then said she was prepared to walk down herself so that they only had to pay for one. But when she was told there was no charge, she stayed on board for the hurl.

POET Angus Peter Campbell, who was in Oban to unveil his first Gaelic novel during the National Mod, was telling folk about the young computer salesman who telephoned an Oban hotel and asked the landlady if he could speak to her IT specialist. But the lady of the house told him, 'No, sorry. We haven't done high teas for years.'

GUIDE in the Royal Scottish Museum: 'These Egyptian carvings are more than 3,000 years old. Perhaps Moses saw them when he was a boy.' English visitor: 'I never knew Moses had been to Edinburgh.'

PATRICK Nellis once worked in a Dunkeld hotel bar where things got so busy that a young lassie from the kitchens was called upon to assist. An American woman approached her, saying, 'Can I have a liqueur coffee?' The girl vanished, returning with a vast catering-industry tin of Nescafé which she brandished in the woman's face as if displaying a bottle of fine wine. The girl had of course mis-heard the US tourist's request as, 'Can I have a look at your coffee?'

HUNGARIAN Szalay Tamas is a fan of Scotland, with a thistle tattooed on his shoulder. He's also written a book about his Scottish visits, the sale of which will raise funds for a children's charity in his homeland. Szalay was once marooned overnight in Glasgow without money, bravely choosing to doze alfresco in George Square. Unsurprisingly, he met various interesting locals. One was very drunk and direct from a pub brawl. Dabbing his bloodied nose, the inebriated Glaswegian chatted matily to Szalay, eventually asking where he came from. 'Hungary,' Szalay replied, whereupon the battered drunk vanished, returning with chicken soup and sandwiches.

A GLASGOW taxi driver swears it is true that when one of his colleagues was hired to take an American tourist on a sightseeing trip to Loch Lomond, the driver got so fed up with the tourist bragging about how much better his own country was at everything that when they parked at Loch Lomond, the driver told him as he gazed out at the loch, 'Well, if you can suck as much as you can blow, you can take it home with you.'

AN American who arrived at Glasgow Airport by taxi from the city centre was telling the check-in staff that she had asked the driver, 'Does the sun ever shine in this country?' And he had told her, 'I don't know. I'm only 28.'

A FURTHER tale of Glasgow taxi drivers coping with the bad weather. A tourist last week making conversation with such a driver remarked, 'Does it always rain here?' 'Naw,' replied the driver, with a lengthy pause before adding, 'Sometimes it snaws.' Is the Taxi Owners' Association sending them to stand-up classes?

TWO German tourists in Glasgow, keen to experience malt whisky for the first time, are directed to the Pot Still in Hope Street, which has one of the city's biggest malt selections. They are drawn to the malt of the month, a ten-year-old Glenmorangie, but the bottle on the bar is empty. Barmaid Linda is about to descend to the cellar when she spots a replacement high on the shelves. Alas, she is unaware that this is merely a display bottle full of nothing but coloured water. And so she pours the two measures.

The Germans, careful with alcohol, gingerly fill the glass with the same again in water, and sip away. A regular, seeing the supposed Glenmorangie drowned, explains they should pour in just a drop to open up the flavour. This they do with their second round of coloured water, and declare it much improved. Fortunately, on their third round, they offer to buy their new friend a dram, and the look on his face at first sip readily identifies the problem with the whisky. The evening ended with the two Germans, fuelled by their replacement drinks, a free shot from the bar and a drink from their new friend, weaving unsteadily towards their hotel and declaring their undying love of malt whisky.

A BOOKSHOP near Waverley Station, full of the usual tartan souvenirs, was busier than ever during the Edinburgh Festival. One American picked up one of the Scottish Saltire tea-towels on show, looked at it for some time, then approached the till and said, 'Gee, this is real nice. Do you have it in red?'

WE have some sympathy for the Americans overheard on the train to Inverness by Martin Anderson of Alford. They were studying a map of Britain and were puzzled at the travelling time between Edinburgh and Inverness – four and a half hours – being the same as the time between London and Edinburgh, although only half the distance. Says Martin, 'Not being aware of the poor state of the rail services north of the border they came to the only possible logical conclusion, i.e. that Inverness was in a different time zone to the rest of the country.'

AMERICAN tourists continued. A group descended from a bus at Glasgow's Botanic Gardens, where one of them took a seat on a bench. 'Where are you from?' asked the local woman sitting next to her, making conversation. 'Arizona,' said the tourist, who then asked where the lady on the bench had come from. 'Doon the road,' she replied, to which the puzzled tourist asked, 'What country is that?'

MOSES IN EDINBURGH

A GROUP of Egyptian students in Glasgow wished to have their picture taken. A passer-by offered to help and collected five cameras from the visitors so that everyone would have a copy. The good Samaritan then asked, 'Is this your first visit to Glasgow?' When the students answered in the affirmative, he told them, 'Well, you'd better get used to this, then,' before haring off round the corner with the cameras. Fortunately, as the puzzled students stood there, the chap reappeared, still laughing at his humorous routine. Ah, the Glasgow banter.

AMERICAN singer Joni Mitchell once arrived at Edinburgh's Doric Tavern with her entourage, who were the worse for drink. When the manager suggested they were a bit rowdy, a punch was thrown by someone in the group and the lot of them were ordered out. Perhaps it was the first time Joni had heard the time-honoured phrase, 'You're barred!' Some time later, a large group of Americans came in to dine at the Doric and when the manager asked how they had heard of the establishment, he was told, 'You're in a guidebook for throwing Joni Mitchell out.' Scottish hospitality: second to none.

ST PATRICK's Day in Dublin saw the usual bearded accordion players busking to cash in on the passing hordes of tourists, many of them from America. One chap, who had lurched out of a pub, watched the entertainers for a while before rooting around in some rubbish. He produced a plastic bucket and two bits of wood, then, to the delight of a group of Americans, sat down, turned the bucket over and began banging on it with the sticks. The delighted tourists tossed euros in his direction until he judged he had enough, threw the bucket away and adjourned to the pub again.

A DAFT joke from St Patrick's Day? Well, what about the American tourist in Limerick who bought the skull of St Patrick in an antique shop for 200 punts. What clinched it for him was a certificate of authenticity signed by St Patrick himself. But visiting the island again ten years later he was shocked to see that the antique shop had another, larger skull in the window purporting to be that of St Patrick. In high dudgeon, he went in and challenged the shop owner, who told him, 'Ah, the one you bought was St Patrick when he was a lad.'

TWELVE

The cry was no defenders

FOOTBALL still has a vice-like grip on the Scottish psyche, although more and more Diary stories are coming from the armchair rather than the park as increasingly it is a satellite rental rather than a pie and a Bovril which collects the cash these days. And it is sitting in your armchair that you hear gems such as footballer-turned-pundit Alan Brazil telling his audience, 'Sir Alex Ferguson IS Manchester United. Cut him and he'd bleed red.'

RADIO Clyde has added to the attractions at the Scottish Football Museum at Hampden by installing phone booths from the old Hampden press box where you can pick up phones and hear memorable recordings from the 30 years of Clyde's *Superscoreboard*. Clyde's Paul Cooney says one of his favourite reports was the hapless pundit in Aberdeen who was giving a half-time resumé at Pittodrie when he suddenly announced in an excited voice, 'And there's trouble here on the pitch, where someone has run on to the park and is being chased by a police dog, and . . . oh my God! . . . his arm has come off!' It was then that someone gently explained to the reporter it was a half-time display by Grampian Police's dog-handlers.

RADIO Scotland's *The Arts Show* was guest-produced by former Scotland winger Pat Nevin, whose long-time interest in film, literature and painting wasn't always shared by his fellow players. Indeed, while reading *The Short Stories of Anton Chekhov* on the Chelsea team bus, Pat was once approached by midfielder Dale Jasper, who remarked, 'At last, Pat! You're reading a book by someone I've heard of – but I didn't know you were a Trekkie.'

FOOTBALL pundit and ex-Man United boss Ron Atkinson was due in at the BBC's Pebble Mill studio to be interviewed for the series *Footballers' Lives* about his views on former Scotland player Andy Gray. At the security desk, he had to fill in a visitor's badge which had spaces for Name, Company, and Visiting. Which is why Big Ron was walking about the studios with a badge which read: 'Name: Ron Atkinson. Company: Pleasant. Visiting: Yes.'

ANDY Kerr in Paisley tells us that his sister was walking along Prospecthill Road in Glasgow just before the Scottish Cup final when she saw four Celtic fans approaching three traffic wardens who were clustered together. The fans piped up with a chorus of 'What a bloody awful job, what a bloody awful job,' although it might have been even more demotic than that. There was a pause, then the traffic wardens chanted back, 'Fifteen pounds an hour, we're making fifteen pounds an hour.'

BEFORE going away to be auctioned for charity, renowned artist Peter Howson's new painting of Celtic legend Henrik Larsson needed framing. A minion went round to collect it from Peter's Glasgow studio, carrying the 3 ft by 4 ft portrait out into nearby Maryhill Road and attempting to hail a taxi. Having successfully flagged down a black hack, the minion opened its rear door and began struggling through, holding the picture out in front of him. The taxi driver took one look at Peter's rendering of Henrik celebrating a goal with gaping mouth and outstretched arms, and immediately roared, 'There's no way that bastard's gettin' in ma cab,' before driving off.

PARTICK Thistle apprentice player Adam Strachan was sent out to see if the undersoil heating at Firhill was working. This would normally be done by digging your studs into the ground but Adam rather genteelly felt the pitch with his hand. This so amused Jags bosses Gerry Britton and Derek Whyte that when the 17 year old shouted he couldn't feel any heat, they turned and addressed a mythical boilerman, crying, 'George, George! You'll need to turn it up,' before returning to Adam and telling him, 'Can you feel it now, son?' The penny eventually dropped after young Adam had been dispatched to gauge heat-levels at all four corner flags.

BBC Radio Scotland's *Sportsound* staff particularly enjoyed it when outspoken presenter Jim Traynor took a post-match call from a very young lad who was giving his opinion of his club's performance that day. As the youngster made his point, Jim tried to put it in perspective by reminding him what the score was at that point in the game. 'You were drawing at the time?' suggested Jim. 'No,' cried the indignant young caller, 'I was at the match.'

AT a St Johnstone v. Motherwell Cup tie, with the 'Well cruising to victory, fans' thoughts were turning to the nightmare that is getting out of the car park at McDiarmid Park. Graham Faulkner overheard two fans discussing the problem, with one opining, 'The car park's always a nightmare – will we leave early and beat the traffic?' 'We came in the supporters' bus, ya eejit,' was the exasperated reply.

NORMAN Wilson tells us of some friends who play at the Pitz five-a-side pitches in Glasgow who, despite their advancing years and waist sizes, had won the Sunday night league. Ready to defend their title, the lads wished to acknowledge the star presence of two Turkish asylum-seekers in their pool of players by renaming themselves Gallusfatterguys.

RANGERS fans were fine ambassadors for their club in Manchester, or so it seems from a message posted on an Ibrox-minded website by Mancunian publican Jay, mein host at The Queen Anne, Ashton Old Road: 'Thanks to you all for treating the pub as your own. Please feel free to pop in any time when you're back down here as you're more than welcome. Apart from the best takings I've ever had, it was my most memorable day as a landlord. PS: I don't give a toss about the window.'

IT will surprise no one to learn that a Tartan Army foot-soldier hired one of Amsterdam's infamous shop-window prostitutes for 30 minutes before the Netherlands–Scotland game. However, upon handing over his cash and being asked, 'What service do you require, sir?' the Scotland fan merely told the woman to go and have a cup of tea. Removing his Scotland shirt, the bulky supporter then took the woman's perch in the window for half an hour, pouting at passing supporters while coyly hoicking his kilt an inch or two above the knee.

TWO Celtic fans from Ayrshire secured tickets from a tout at the last minute for the Parkhead game against Bayern Munich – but they were for the small section set aside for Bayern supporters. So, carefully not wearing anything green, which might give them away, they approached the turnstiles. However, an alert security chap sensed that all might not be well and asked the first lad where he was from. He gave a puzzled look, shrugged his shoulders, and spoke gibberish in a guttural accent which he hoped was a close enough approximation of German. Sadly, his pal, clearly not a fan of the film *The Great Escape*, was asked a similar question and replied, 'Saltcoats. Why?' Which is why he ended up watching the game in a nearby pub.

JIM Buchan recalls attending the 1986 Aberdeen–Hearts Scottish Cup final with his dad and brother. As the Buchans took their centre-stand seats, a pipe band marched up and down Hampden's hallowed turf. Being from Montrose, Jim's dad revelled in the chance to celebrity-spot. A famous comedian was to the trio's left, a TV commentator to the right. When told that Gordon Strachan, who wasn't playing that day, was sitting behind them, Jim's dad couldn't contain himself. He turned, saying, 'Aye aye, Gordon, do you no' wish you were out there this afternoon?' Gordon deadpanned, 'Naw. Ah cannae play the bagpipes.'

WE were taken with the Tartan Army fan in Dortmund, interviewed on Radio Scotland's *Fred MacAulay Show*, who was asked by Fred if it was apparent from the terraces that the German players were guilty of diving. 'Yes,' said the chap laconically. 'We did wonder why the German team came out wearing Speedos.'

IT'S not true, of course, but some traditionalists claim that football and girlfriends don't mix. Reader Martin Tierney tells us of a Celtic season-ticket holder who took his girlfriend along when his mate in the next seat couldn't make it to a game. Enjoying the mirthful possibilities of saying whatever she liked, the perspicacious girlfriend loudly observed, when Henrik Larsson led the team out holding the hand of that day's seven-year-old mascot, that 'young Shaun Maloney looks larger on the telly'.

DURING Rangers' break in Dubai, a fans' forum was arranged for the 100-plus members of the newly formed Dubai Loyal. Attended by several players, including Ibrox captain Lorenzo Amoruso, the event's question-and-answer session provoked only anodyne enquiries from the floor, prompting the MC to conclude matters with a request for one final question. A startlingly direct query ensued, aimed at Lorenzo Amoruso: 'How much do you earn?' Lorenzo declined to answer. The question had been cheekily voiced by Lorenzo's teammate, Fernando Ricksen.

DURING the live pay-per-view TV coverage of a game between Hibernian and Rangers, commentator Jock Brown expressed dismay at Easter Road's sparse attendance. 'A disappointing crowd,' Jock opined. 'I'd have thought more folk would be here for such an attractive fixture.' Jock's match-summariser, ex-Hibee Darren Jackson, supportively proffered his opinion. 'It hardly helps,' Darren noted, 'that the game's being televised.'

CELTIC skipper Paul Lambert was lining up a golf shot behind the goal at Celtic Park for photographers as part of a promotion to attract more golfers to Scotland. When they had finished snapping, he unleashed a drive which thundered off a seat in the top tier of the Jock Stein Stand opposite. As if the shot itself wasn't impressive enough, Paul pointed at the seat he had hit and remarked, 'That guy gives me stick every week.' Someone trying to work out the distance asked Paul, 'Is the park 110 yards long?' 'Aye, but it's 140 yards long when you're getting a doing,' replied Lambert the philosopher.

GIVEN Iceland's seafaring heritage, it was perhaps inevitable that at their game against Scotland the Tartan Army would break into a chorus of, 'You're fish, and you know you are.'

A PEEK at the viewers' complaints log at Scottish Television where several objected to a sports headline on the screen about Rangers Football Club, claiming it was encouraging bigotry and sectarianism. An injury crisis at the club was headlined as, 'The cry was no defenders'.

GOOD to report that there are still fanatics supporting the less fashionable Scottish football teams. On a St Mirren fans' website it is reported that two such devotees finished work on a Tuesday at 5 p.m. and decided to travel to the club's Bell's Challenge Cup match against Ross County up in Dingwall. Still on the road at half-time, they got a text message telling them St Mirren were losing. Then a second text message to tell them of an equaliser, then extra time, but they were still not at the ground. Finally, after getting lost in Inverness, they reached the stadium and burst in during the penalty shoot-out decider, watched seven penalties, then drove south again. As one of them told the website, 'If only every game was like that – missing out the p*** bits, see seven kicks of a ball, and Saints winning.'

THIRTEEN

Plain speaking

NOW there is nothing a Scotsman in the world of business likes better than to don the dinner suit, sit back amongst a table of colleagues, let the wine and spirits flow, and hear a good after-dinner speaker. Broadcaster Dougie Donnelly once claimed in fact that his daughter wondered whether he was allergic to his dinner jacket as it always made him feel sick the morning after he had been wearing it.

AFTER-DINNER speaker John McKelvie from Motherwell was entertaining the troops at Clyde Football Club's annual dinner when he was asked how he managed to stay sober when he was plied with drink at such events. 'No bother,' he replied. 'I just keep a photograph of a North Lanarkshire councillor in my top pocket – and once his face looks honest, I know I've had too much to drink.'

FORMER Glasgow Lord Provost Alex Mosson was at his cheeky best when presenting a community service award to Sister Teresa O'Neil for her years of selfless dedication to the sick and needy of Glasgow's Blackhill. The Franciscan sister gave Alex a peck on the

Private dentists guilty of ripping off patients face being struck off

cheek when she got her award, so Alex kissed her back, then cheerfully announced, 'A wee kiss on a nun's cheek is allowed – as long as you don't get into the habit.'

MURDO MacLeod, the football commentator, was recalling his days as a player at Celtic at the Beanfeast children's charity dinner in Glasgow. Before one particular Old Firm game, manager Billy McNeill divided the players into Protestants and Catholics for the five-a-sides, and to make the numbers up, swapped Bobby Lennox over to the Protestant team. As all the players were competing for a place in Saturday's side, they were all up for it, with Bobby getting some harsh treatment. After being sent sprawling for the second or third time, Bobby turned to Murdo and told him, 'Ah've only been a Protestant for 20 minutes and already ah hate those Fenian so-and-sos.' And he may not have said so-and-sos.

COMEDIAN and lifelong Rangers fan Andy Cameron was acting as auctioneer at a charity event. About to start the bidding for a signed Celtic top, Andy quietly asked fellow top-table guest, former Ranger Mark Hateley, to do him a favour and start the bidding at a reasonable level so he could get a fair show for the top. Mark agreed, loudly shouting out, '£300!' Equally loudly, Andy cried, 'Sold!'

OUTGOING Glasgow City Council chief executive Jimmy Andrews, in his farewell speech, was recalling his time as finance director. Jimmy said he once received a polite letter from a worried woman saying she'd lost her poll tax paying-in book. 'I don't want to fall behind,' she wrote, 'and so I wonder if you could send me a new book.' The letter ended with an unexpected PS: 'Don't bother with a new book, I've just found the old one.'

MUCH-TRAVELLED football manager Tommy Docherty was chatting with a researcher before appearing on Tam Cowan's BBC programme *Offside* when the researcher told him that he was a Falkirk supporter. 'Falkirk,' replied Tommy wistfully. 'I've often said that if I won the lottery I'd buy Falkirk.' As the researcher stammered in disbelief, Tommy continued, 'Of course, when I tell folk this, they always say to me, "But what would you do if you got four numbers?"' Tommy's storytelling has, of course, made him a star of the after-dinner speaking circuit. One of our favourite Docherty stories is when he was talking warmly about the late, and much missed, no-nonsense Scotland defender, Jim Holton. Tommy recalled, 'When Jim was at Man United we put bells on a football so he would know where it was. We had complaints from morris dancers saying he was kicking them all over the place.'

HARLEQUIN Leisure boss Charan Gill, of Ashoka restaurants fame, was named Asian Entrepreneur of the Year at a ceremony in London, where he explained that his success was only possible because of Glaswegians' passion for curries – in fact, one of the Ashoka regulars decided to name his children after his favourite dishes. Said Charan, 'His wife, of course, wasn't very pleased, but their first born was a wee girl – so he called her Patty because he liked *patia*. And he liked some *raita* with it, so he called the second one Rita. The third one, of course, just had to be Nan. By this time, his wife thought this was a good idea and decided to name the next child after her favourite dish. So, if you're ever in Glasgow and you bump into a sad-looking guy called Chicken Tikka McDonald, you'll know he doesn't love his mother.'

DOUGIE Donnelly, presenting *The Dram* magazine's Scottish Licensed Trade Awards, explained the realities of fame. Walking down Glasgow's Buchanan Street, he was stopped by two wifies, one of whom grabbed his arm and said, 'It's you, isn't it?' Tentatively, Dougie agreed that he was indeed himself. At that, the second lady chimed in, 'Aye, it's him.' Just as Dougie wondered whether he should get the pen out to sign an autograph or two, the first woman came back with, 'When are you coming back to finish my bathroom?'

LOVEABLE rascal Frank McAvennie, the ex-Celtic and West Ham star, was reminiscing at the launch of his book, *Scoring: An Expert's Guide*, about the time he and fellow scallywag Mo Johnston were caught by an SFA official sneaking into the Scottish team's Glasgow hotel at four in the morning – way past curfew time. Unfortunately, Mo thought the blazered chap was the night porter and tried to push a tenner into his top pocket. It was only then that Frank noticed the SFA badge on the outraged official's blazer. When news of their offence became public, the BBC sent sports reporter Chick Young to interview Frank and, full of establishment wrath, Chick asked what they were thinking about being in the Warehouse discothèque when they should have been preparing for a game. Frank's reply of, 'You tell us,

Chick, as you were still in the Warehouse when we left,' was never broadcast.

A SPEAKER at a dinner in Glasgow posed the question, 'Where would we be without laughter?' A chap in front of him shouted out, 'Edinburgh.'

PARLIAMENTARIAN Tony Benn showed he was as sharp as ever when addressing an audience at Paisley University. Tony opined that prime minister's questions at Westminster should be renamed gardeners' question time – because so many of them are planted.

BBC Scotland news queen Jackie Bird, at a corporate awards bash at the Glasgow Hilton, targeted the event's VIP guest of honour, Jack McConnell, the first minister. 'Jack and his government colleagues are staging a Christmas panto,' Jackie declared. 'Enterprise minister Jim Wallace will play Wishy-Washy – because he is,' said Jackie, and she went on to say that Jack's own role would be Buttons, as 'buttons will be all that's left after we've paid for the new parliament building'.

JOHN Reid, the health secretary, speaking at a Labour fund-raiser at Glasgow's Hilton, attended by Tony Blair, was recounting being appointed to his previous job, Northern Ireland secretary. He said that as a lad from Clydeside, he was quite surprised by the opulence of his office accommodation in a former palace. Said John, 'I had just arrived when the butler – butler, mind you – tells me we have urgent matters to discuss. He asks to meet me in 15 minutes in the throne room. So there I was, standing for 15 minutes . . . outside the bog.' John was also impressed that the *Titanic* was built in Belfast, and was in excellent condition when it sailed. 'I rather suspect that when the Prods were building the *Titanic* in west Belfast, the Catholics were very busy in the east of the city. Making the iceberg.'

GLASGOW-BASED author Bernard MacLaverty, musing on the often strained relationship between writers and publishers, gave the example of the frustrated novelist who'd sent a manuscript to Faber & Faber, only to have it rejected. According to Bernard, the would-be literary giant tried to make light of things by saying he'd been assured Faber had loved his book – but then Faber had said he hated it.

IF comedy is all about timing, then spare a thought for Dunfermline Football Club director Jim Leishman, who had just stood up to deliver the Toast to the Lassies at a charity Burns Supper in Edinburgh when the Sheraton Hotel's fire alarm went off. The hundreds of guests quietly trooped outside into the Edinburgh gloom for 10 or 15 minutes before the all-clear was given and they dutifully returned to their seats. At that, Jim, back at the microphone, waited for them to settle, before announcing, 'So in conclusion, ladies and gentlemen . . .'

OLYMPIC gold-medal runner Roger Black, who gave an inspiring speech at Glasgow City Council's Sportsperson of the Year awards dinner, admitted that he was not much of a joke-teller. He then went on to say that he was sitting next to David Beckham at a similar dinner when the waitress asked David if he liked scampi. The footballing maestro told her that, not only did he like scampi, but he enjoyed all the Disney films.

FOURTEEN

Competition time

THE most humbling part of working on The Diary is realising how much sharper than us the readers are. We often put them to the test with competitions, and they never let us down. We asked them to update the endings of sayings and proverbs, and they suggested:

- A stitch in time . . . means that NHS waiting lists are coming down after all. (Gordon Peden)
- If you can't beat them . . . what's the point of having children? (Marian Russell, Dunfermline)
- You win some you . . . don't support Scotland. (Charlie Thomson, Glasgow)
- If you can't stand the heat . . . you're abroad. (Ken Dagger)
- If you can't stand the heat . . . you're probably not going to like *Hello!* much either. (Ross McKay)
- Red sky in morning . . . you're wearing the wean's sunglasses. (Tommy Fowler)
- Too many cooks . . . spoil the television schedules. (Almost everyone)

COMPETITION TIME

- If you don't have something nice to say . . . go on reality TV. (Brian Cherry)
- There's many a slip . . . in M&S's lingerie department. (Alex Johnston, Garrowhill)
- It ain't over till . . . Michelle McManus. (Dr Kiain Balloch, High Blantyre)
- Practice makes . . . banjo players' neighbours move. (Gordon Campbell, Bearsden)
- An Englishman's home is . . . full of redundant St George's flags. (Rosie Gallagher, Birmingham)
- There's no such thing as a free . . . kitchen. (John McMillan)
- A fool and his money . . . will try to help Chelsea win the Premiership. (Andy McLellan)
- See a pin . . . don't pick it up, it might be a junkie's needle. (Tom Donnelly, Hyndland)
- An apple a day . . . crashes. (David Thomas, Bothwell)
- It is better to travel hopefully . . . when on the M8. (John Edwards, Linlithgow)
- Look before you . . . join the queue at Ikea. (Paul Kerr)
- There is many a true word . . . omitted by a politician. (Dan Harris, Chryston)
- We'll cross that bridge . . . when the toll's abolished. (Jim Smith, East Kilbride)

- Many a mickle . . . be over on the Seacat. (John McMillan)
- Two's company, three's a . . . dearer round. (Ian Wilson)
- If at first you don't succeed . . . become a list MSP. (Peter McGuinness, Garelochhead)
- How green was my . . . PM. (Lex Johnston)
- You scratch my back . . . and my wife will scratch your eyes out. (David McMillan).

THEN word came that the Scottish Executive were spending thousands of pounds to come up with an advertising slogan for Scotland. *Herald* readers, naturally, would do it merely in the hope of winning a bottle of whisky:

- Scotland – it's nice sometimes in May. (Ali Clark, Milngavie)
- Scotland – we border on the unacceptable. (Ali Clark, Milngavie)
- Scotland – It's Miles of Batter. (Ali Clark, Milngavie)
- Welcome to Scotland. Sorry About the Mess. (Ali Clark, Milngavie)
- Scotland. We shellsuit you! (Ali Clark, Milngavie)
- Scotland 0 – everyone else at least 3. (Dave Head, Baillieston)
- Scotland – new parliament to support, please give generously. (Graham Birse)
- Scotland – Carlsberg don't make countries, but if they did, we'd still drink Tennent's. (Dr Kiain Balloch, High Blantyre)
- Like *The Big Issue*? You'll love Scotland! (Rhona-Mairead Sweeting)
- Scotland – proudly preventing English independence since 1707. (Duncan Kerr, Linlithgow)
- Scotland – so good that Sean Connery occasionally visits. (Anne Keane)

COMPETITION TIME

- Scotland – who swears wins. (David Watt)
- Scotland – raining world champions. (Doug McVitie, France)

WE challenged the '60s baby boomers, now feeling their age, to update their favourite songs. Here is a selection of their suggestions:

- Carly Simon – 'You're So Varicose Vein' (Michael Brown)
- The Rolling Stones – 'You Can't Always Pee When You Want' (Michael Brown)
- The Temptations – 'Papa's Got a Kidney Stone' (Michael Brown)
- Leo Sayer – 'You Make Me Feel Like Napping' (Michael Brown)
- The Commodores – 'Once, Twice, Three Trips to the Bathroom' (Michael Brown)
- Cliff Richard – 'We Don't Walk Anymore' (Eddie Kelman)
- Rod Stewart – 'Do You Think I'm Sixty?' (Stuart Cosgrove)
- Led Zeppelin – 'Stairlift to Heaven' (Annie White)
- Frank Ifield – 'I Remember . . . Who?' (David Walker, Kilmacolm)
- Jeff Beck – 'Hi-Ho Fleecy Lining' (Robert Kerr, East Kilbride)
- Dave Edmunds – 'I Hear You Chappin'' (Colin Agnew, Burnside)
- The Kinks – 'Wantheloo Now Pet' (Colin Kerr, Glasgow)
- Steve Harley & Cockney Rebel – 'Come Up and See Me (Make My Tea)' (Brian Scobie, Prestwick)
- Diana Ross – 'Do You Know Where I'm Going To?' (Bert Houliston, Cumbria)

- Ian Dury – 'Hit Me With Your Walking Stick' (Lynda Wallace, Kilmarnock)
- Gerry and The Pacemakers – 'Sherry Down Yer Jersey' (Bill Martin, Croftamie)
- Rolling Stones – '(Hey You) Get Offa My Commode' (Robert Gilhooly)
- Meat Loaf – 'You Took the Teeth Right Out of My Mouth' (Angela Paterson, Cambuslang)
- Bob Dylan – 'The Pads, They Need a Changin'' (Jimmy Milroy, Bearsden)
- The Beatles – 'Bad Back' (Kenny Mackay, Skye)
- Lovin' Spoonful – 'Zimmer in the City' (Paul Kerr)
- The Beatles – 'Love Me Doos' (Jacqueline Houston)
- Chubby Checker – 'Let's Whist Again' (Jacqueline Houston)

- Lulu – 'Gout!' (Unknown of Portree)
- Petula Clark – 'Downhill' (Frank Croft, Paisley)
- Jimi Hendrix – 'Purple Hair' (Linda Menzies, Edinburgh)
- John Travolta and Olivia Newton-John – 'You're The Scone That I Want' (Andrew Campbell, Hamilton).
- Long John Baldry – 'Let the Backaches Begin' (Steve Gibbs, Neilston)
- Shirelles – 'Will You Still Know Me Tomorrow?' (Craig Spence, Glasgow)
- Status Quo – 'Rockin' All Over the Ward' (Neil Macleod, Beauly)
- Julie London – 'Buy Me a Liver' (Tam Balloch, Glasgow)
- Bad Company – 'Feel Like Makin' Lunch' (Allan Kelly, Perth)
- Neil Sedaka – 'Raking Up is Hard to Do' (Philip Graham, Knightswood)
- The Who – 'I Can't Sit for Piles' (John Morrison, Kilbarchan)
- Middle of the Road – 'Hirple Hirple Creak Creak' (J. Brown, Cumbernauld)
- Manfred Mann – '5–4–3–2–HOUSE!' (Alan Stewart, Glasgow)

FOR Christmas, we wanted definitions of words updated, and suggested:

- Gregarious – meeting your pals in the lunch-time queue at the bakery.
- Tantalising – entertaining one's aunt in the hope of a postal order.
- Barbecue – joining in the desperate last-minute rush for this year's must-have Christmas toy for girls.

The readers came back with:

- Brillo pad – young Kelvinsider describes her new flat in the West End. (John Kelly)
- Brouhaha – jokes about our other national drink. (Davie McCloy)
- Remit – to put on woolly gloves again. (Gordon Cubie)
- Digimon – request for confirmation of questionable sexual endeavours. (Patrick Quinn)
- Embarrassed – feeling of discomfort when arrested in possession of pirate-copy DVDs at Glasgow's famous east-end market. (Stuart Crawford)
- Fitment – the ultimate question about life's purpose, as asked by folk in Stonehaven. (Bill O'Donnell)
- Rigmarole – to have something dishonest done to your small, round, individually baked piece of bread. (Mark Hillan)
- Condescending – Jeffrey Archer's progress down the stairs. (Gerry Hastings)
- Embrocation – special event taking place at the M8's eastern end. (Bill Martin)
- Fundamentalist – register of persons enraged by the negative performance of their pension funds. (Bert Houliston)
- Ruth – what you tell your partner after the office Christmas night out (i.e., not the whole truth). (Donald Hunter)
- Assegai – perhaps that gentleman can help us. (Tom Donnelly, Hyndland)
- Microwave – perm for a wee wumman. (W. Thompson, Glasgow)
- Acoustic – cattle prod. (Lynn Hughes, Cyprus)
- Catholic – someone who is addicted to owning cats. (David McCloy)
- Metaphor – previously encountered in Glasgow. (Patrick Kelly, Paisley)
- Emeritus – clergyman who officiated at our wedding. (R Simpson, Paisley)

- Larceny – art of winning by a last-minute penalty at Parkhead. (Donnie MacNeill, Livingston)
- Claustrophobia – fear of meeting old chap with white beard in a chimney. (Carl Williamson, Largs)
- Freemasonry – bricks nicked from a building site. (Jim Cook, Airdrie)
- Ineffable – celibate lady. (Russell Campbell)
- Hispanic – pregnancy test. (Jan Brown)
- Linoleum – Croy family debate over the girl's or boy's name for their next wean. (Kenny Reid)
- Penitent – cheap camping equipment. (Stephen Gold)
- Metronome – a wee man on the Paris underground. (Joyce Orr)
- Effluent – having a wide command of abusive language. (Tom Donnelly)
- Negligent – undergarment worn by transvestites. (Robert Jenkins)
- Wishy-washy – Lanarkshire launderette. (Patrick Kelly, Paisley)
- Cauterize – she noticed me. (Ian Barnett, Newton Mearns)
- Lingerie – time passing slowly for the prime minister's wife. (June Falconer)
- First footer – preliminary grope. (Jimmy Campbell)
- Generous – buying your Christmas presents at a well-known Edinburgh store. (Nita Marr, Longniddry)
- Trinket – mischievous exhortations at a Hogmanay party. (Andrew Campbell)

WE all have our favourite films. But what is the line that would have killed a cherished film stone dead if it had been muttered halfway through? What would have happened to *Psycho* if Norman Bates had said to the Janet Leigh character, 'I'm sorry, but the shower's not working.' Or if Captain Smith on the bridge of the *Titanic* had opined, 'Pretty warm for this time of year.' Our readers suggested:

- *The Italian Job* – Charlie Croker to coach driver: 'Slow down, you nearly went off the road there!' (Hugh Parker)
- *Death Wish* – Charles Bronson: 'I hope the police can find the killers.' (Joe Mullan, Hong Kong)
- *Saving Private Ryan* – Chief of Staff: 'Find me James Ryan.' Reply: 'Sorry, sir. He's already dead.' (Joe Mullan, Hong Kong)
- *High Noon* – 'Damn – that old clock's gone and stopped again.' (Bill Robertson, Eaglesham)
- *Braveheart* – William Wallace: 'I have a sneaking admiration for the English.' (Barry Hunter)
- *Gregory's Girl* – 'Sir, can we girls play netball?' (Moira and Eilidh Paterson)
- *Twelve Angry Men* – Juror No. 8: 'OK, you've all convinced me, I want to change my vote to guilty.'
- *It's a Wonderful Life* – George Bailey: 'That's a very fair offer, Mr Potter, the Building and Loan is now yours.'
- *Rear Window* – L.B. 'Jeff' Jeffries: 'Look at the new blinds all my neighbours have just had installed.'
- *Star Wars* – Darth Vader: 'I'm not going to fight you, Luke; come and give your old man a big hug.' (Kenny Mathieson, Edinburgh)
- *Fatal Attraction* – Michael Douglas: 'I'm sorry, I can't – I'm married.' (Calum Walker)
- *Greyfriars Bobby* – Finlay Currie: 'When I die, shoot the dog and bury him with me.' (Jim Thomson)
- *The Sound of Music* – Maria: 'You're right, Mother Superior, my place is here and not with these horrid children.' (Isobel Law)
- *Waiting for Godot* – 'Godot – you're early.' (Barney Macfarlane)
- *Casablanca* – Rick's Bar doorman to Ingrid Bergman: 'Sorry, hen, regulars only the night.' (Robert Kirkwood)
- *Spartacus* – 'Yes, he's Spartacus.' (Gail Wylie)

- *Kramer v. Kramer* – '. . . and take the boy with you.' (Peter Kaminski)
- *Mrs Doubtfire* – 'Dad, why are you dressed like that?' (Paul Kerr)
- *Last Tango in Paris* – 'What's this? Low-cholesterol, low-fat sunflower spread? Ah, forget it.' (Ian Duff)
- *Chariots of Fire* – 'Mr Liddell, about your urine sample . . .' (Jim Palmer)
- *Marathon Man* – 'These new false teeth of mine are great.' (Doug High)
- *Saturday Night Fever* – 'Aw, Mum, you've washed red socks with my good white trousers.' (Kay Cowan)

AND can you guess the following?

- 'Pongo, who's going to the vet today? Good boy.' (Mark Johnston)
- 'Fly Spitfires? With these legs? It's a desk job I want.' (David McVey)
- 'What do you mean you gave the ring to the big man in black?' (Andy Campbell)
- 'Sarnt-Major, that's the machine guns in place.' (Andy Burns)
- 'I had it here somewhere.' (Bob Mitchell)
- 'Phew, that's a relief, the doctor says it's just a bit of a cold.' (Alistair from The Jaggy Thistle)
- 'No thanks, I'll stand.' (Ian Johnstone)

They were, of course, *101 Dalmatians, Reach for the Sky, Lord of the Rings, Zulu, Schindler's List, Love Story* and *Basic Instinct*.

FIFTEEN

Banjo player's blonde

IT may no longer be Lex McLean telling old Rangers jokes at the *Five Past Eight Show* in a Glasgow theatre. Entertainment is far more international now, with acts arriving in Scotland from around the world for the Edinburgh Festival, Celtic Connections in Glasgow or various jazz, folk and contemporary music festivals. But the smart one-liners are still bellowed out. At a stand-up comedy show in Glasgow, a comedian, dying horribly in front of his non-laughing audience, tried to engage in some audience rapport by asking a chap at the front, 'What do you do for a living?' He mercilessly replied, 'I'm a plumber . . . what do you do?'

TEENAGE violin prodigy Nicola Benedetti from West Kilbride once toured with the Scottish Ensemble. Each night, proceedings began with an avant-garde work in which the band stumbled around the stage, apparently tuning up in conditions alternating between semi-darkness and total blackout. In Edinburgh, clued-up music-lovers listened with rapt attention. In Dundee, however, there was consternation, with one respectable-looking woman in the front row angrily storming out. Her high heels echoing round

98

the auditorium, she snapped, 'For God's sake! I'll fix the bloody lights myself.'

A SCREENING of Mel Gibson's harrowing *The Passion of the Christ* had just ended in a Glasgow cinema when a reader noticed a chap standing up to leave but his partner remaining seated. The chap was obviously worried that she had been overcome with emotion, as he asked, 'Are you all right?' The lady with him replied that she just wanted to remain seated until the credits had finished. Clearly concerned that the relentless violence of the film had affected her, he again asked, 'Are you feeling OK?' At that, she turned to him and said, 'I'm just waiting to see if they do any funny out-takes at the end.'

IT is said that Mick Broderick, the rumbustious former member of the Whistlebinkies traditional music group, visited a friend on Arran unexpectedly but didn't find him in. In desperation, Mick, recalling his pal had a parrot, dropped to his knees and bellowed repeatedly through the letterbox, 'Big Mick. In pub. Five o'clock.' The racket attracted the attention of his pal's neighbour, who looked out of the window, heard what Mick was shouting, and told his pal when he returned. So when the chap did indeed go to the pub to meet Mick at five o'clock, an astonished Mick could only say, 'That's some parrot you've got.'

AND do we believe the chap who said he was in the queue at the popcorn counter at a Glasgow cinema where the bloke in front said, 'Three pounds for popcorn? The last time I was here it was less than a pound.' And the assistant calmly looked at him and said, 'Oh well, you're in for a right treat tonight then. They've added sound.'

READER David Simpson drew our attention to the *Edinburgh Evening News*, where Edinburgh's licensing board chairman, Phil Attridge, complained about too many lap-dancing clubs in the city. Or, as he told the *News*, 'I don't like there being so many in Lothian Road, and so in-your-face.' Quite.

ACTRESS Dorothy Paul, in her autobiography, *Dorothy: Revelations of a Rejected Soprano*, gives us an insight into the early days of Scottish Television. She was asked to appear on a sadly departed 15-minute programme, *The Admag*, which demonstrated new products on a live show. Says Dorothy, 'A new screwdriver was being advertised. This screwdriver could do all sorts of things. The presenter started off well enough. He was standing holding the screwdriver in a kind of threatening pose. "Now, ladies, we're going to look at home improvements and I'm going to show you something that every woman can put up herself." He looked at the screwdriver and nearly fainted with embarrassment.'

ONE for film fans. Comedian Mark Billingham says the best heckle he ever heard was when Eric Douglas, the brother of film star Michael, who has never had his brother's success, attempted to be a stand-up comedian. In a try-out at a London comedy club he was embarrassingly finding no laughs until, frustrated at the audience's lack of interest, he shouted at them, 'Listen, you assholes. Don't you know who I am? I'm Kirk Douglas's son.' At that, a chap in the audience stood up and declared, 'No, I'm Kirk Douglas's son.' Then another chap, cottoning on, stood up and said, 'No, I'm Kirk Douglas's son,' and then a third, and a fourth, until the audience, well, at least the *Spartacus* fans, were helpless with laughter.

APPEARING at Celtic Connections, Nashville veteran Dobro acoustic guitarist Jerry Douglas re-ignited the simmering debate about the relative merits of banjo players. 'What do you call a beautiful blonde on a banjo player's arm?' asked Jerry. The answer? 'A tattoo.'

JAZZ singer Todd Gordon experienced a Glasgow audience when he previewed his Edinburgh Fringe show *The Sinatra Years* in the city's OranMor arts venue. Some friends he invited along to the show were chatting to two women afterwards when one of the ladies said how much she'd enjoyed Todd's performance. 'Aye,' added her friend, 'he isnae Sinatra – but he's no a bag o' pish.' It took a while for Todd to be persuaded that in Glasgow this was, in fact, quite a compliment.

THE Diary has mainly been a *Big Brother*-free zone, but we felt we ought to pass on an observation from Peter Lindsay of Cardonald, who was watching the fifth series of the Channel 4 show with the subtitles on so that he could comprehend 'Portugeezer' Nadia. On the screen was Lanarkshire poseur Jason, who commented, 'That was a master stroke, bronzin' my backside last night.' However, the subtitles, perhaps trying to cope with his glottal stop, came up as: 'That was a master stroke, prawns in my backside last night.'

GLASGOW comedian Raymond Mearns, a regular at the Stand Comedy Club in the city's West End, says the toughest heckler he faced was across the city at a community centre in Easterhouse. Raymond had started a funny monologue about how his wife doesn't do the house-cleaning very well, when a voice fired out from the darkness, 'Then clean it yersel', ya fat bastart.' The logic of that sally left Raymond, for once, speechless. Incidentally, Raymond was touring in the North-east when pilots at the local RAF base invited him back for a nightcap. Raymond was astonished that the guard on duty accepted his Global Video card as proof of identity in these heightened security times. He shouldn't really be surprised, though, as getting a video card these days involves more proofs of identity than you would need to get a passport.

NOSTALGIA website glasgowapollo.com documents the Clash's gig in 1978 when the band, believing erroneously that it was the Apollo's last gig, was worried the bouncers would relish a final opportunity to batter local punk-rock fans. The gig was a tense affair, with the Clash repeatedly asking the warring factions to stop fighting in the stalls. Subsequently, Joe Strummer and Paul Simonon were arrested for being drunk and disorderly, along with numerous fans. Freed from overnight custody, they encountered dancer Lionel Blair in their hotel lobby. Upon hearing their sorry tale of violence and imprisonment, Lionel merely smiled, saying, 'Well, that's show business.'

FAST-TALKING and fast-playing comedy piano-tinkling duo Katzenjammer, appearing at the Edinburgh Fringe, fondly remember an eccentric ventriloquist they appeared with on the same bill. It wasn't unusual, for example, for the artist to be heard from outside his dressing-room having violent disagreements with his plastic pretend friend. The Katzenjammer lads called his hotel room to invite him to lunch in a local Thai restaurant one day. To their surprise, the dummy answered the phone, and in his squeaky voice announced that his partner was otherwise engaged, but he would be happy to accept the invitation on his behalf. The next day, the lads waited an hour at the restaurant for him, but he didn't show, so they phoned the hotel to see where he was. The ventriloquist couldn't apologise enough and seemed to be genuinely embarrassed; the reason he didn't turn up, as he told them, was because the dummy had not passed on the message.

COMEDIAN John Moloney recalls leaving the Gilded Balloon venue at the Edinburgh Fringe one year a bit worse-for-wear with foppish Oxbridge fellow comedian Jeremy Hardy. Outside, Jeremy saw a third performer, Simon Munnery, defacing one of his posters, and took a weak swing at him. Munnery retaliated with a pathetic swing of his arm at Hardy also, which was observed by the officers in a passing police car. All of them were bundled into the car, given a stern warning, and then let out a hundred yards away. They still recall the final admonition of one of the officers: 'That's the trouble with you English bastards – it's all shite and no fight.'

ONE reader recalls that, during the Thatcher years, a comedian started a lengthy monologue about Thatcher turning up at a rail crash, at a building collapse, a school fire and so on. 'Why is it,' continued the struggling comic, 'that whenever there is a disaster, she turns up?' 'So why isn't she here, then?' came the inevitable shout from the audience.

SIXTEEN

Till tales

SHOPPING is still a realm where confusion can reign, as enquiries are misconstrued, and overworked and underpaid staff can perhaps be a little too tart in their replies. At a Dumbarton supermarket for example, a local chap, who thought he was a bit smart with the ladies, tried to cheer up a rather dour-faced assistant with the oft-used line, 'Cheer up! It'll mibbae no' happin.' But she merely fixed him in her gaze and announced, 'The oanly thing cheers me up is knowin' that it'll never happin wi' yoo.'

WE pass on the story of the woman who phoned the George Bowie show on Radio Clyde to explain that she was looking at a second-hand microwave oven in a shop window that was labelled 'ex con'. The woman turned to her friend and declared, 'Imagine selling a microwave that's been in a prison cell.' It was then that her pal gently explained that it only meant it was in excellent condition.

READERS have fond memories of perfume salesgirls who worked at the glamorous edge of retailing. Charles Provan of Larkhall remembers the time he was still dating his future wife and went to

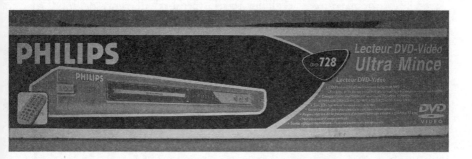

that vast upmarket emporium Frasers in Glasgow's Buchanan Street to buy her a present. He was eyeing up the perfume named Joy but as it was expensive, he asked the glamorous assistant, 'Is this perfume good?' 'Good?' she replied. 'Tell madam not to wear it if she is only bluffing.'

A LEGENDARY Frasers store story, recalled for us by James MacGregor in Perth, is about the late Sir Hugh Fraser strolling through the department store when he still owned it and hearing a girl behind the counter telling a customer, 'You'll get it across the road at Lewis's.' Yes, we're really dragging out the old names here. So, after the customer left, Sir Hugh took the assistant aside and told her she was never to say that again, as the correct response was to say that although it was not in stock she would endeavour to get it, and the customer should call back in a day or so. 'What did she want, anyway?' Hugh asked at the end of his diatribe. 'The bus to Anniesland,' the girl replied.

THE perfume stories reminded Margaret Moore, now in Australia, of the time she ran perfume parties in her younger days back in Glasgow. She tells us: 'Part of the evening was a quiz, with the answers being the names of famous perfumes. On one memorable night, the question came up, 'What would you give your worst enemy?' Most people got the right answer, 'Poison', apart from one who went for the more parochial answer, 'Ma Griffe'.

A MARKET gardener who used hydroponics to produce herbs, which sold extremely well at Perth farmers' market, decided to extend her business by setting up a stall in Dundee. Customers in Dundee, though, were just a tad different from those in Perth, as a young lad looked at her plants and said, 'Is that cannabis you're growing there?' The dear lady followed his finger before gently correcting him with, 'No, that's marjoram. And if it was cannabis, do you honestly think I would be charging just 50p a punnet?'

GLASGOW southsider John Kimble decided to open a chocolate shop in the city's St Enoch Centre and named it Les Cygnes – The Swans – after the brand name of Belgian chocolate makers Kim's, who supply his shop. John now has to spend the day dealing with customers who say things like 'Morning, Les', and 'Thanks very much, Les', and so far he hasn't had the heart to set them straight.

A READER couldn't get over the sunny-dispositioned checkout girl at the express till who stopped an old fellow with a full basket trying to avoid the lengthier queues at the other tills. Pointing to the notice about ten items or fewer, she asked him, 'What is it you have difficulty with – reading or counting?'

READER Lynda Shevlin wrote to us: 'I was recently tasked with purchasing a colander for my daughter to drain the varied dishes of pasta that make up the average diet of many students. I found myself searching the shelves of a local Fife branch of Poundstretchers, but couldn't find a colander anywhere. Time was pressing, so I approached the young assistant and asked her, "Do you have any colanders in stock?" She gave me a rather strange look and in a strong Fife accent said, "Naw, there'll be nae caulanders in till November or December. Hiv ye tried W.H. Smith's? They might hiv some left." I thanked her and left.'

CUSTOMER service, banking style. A reader tells us he was in a queue in a bank in Glasgow and the woman in front was being charged a pound for some service or other when she told the counter-staff indignantly, 'I wasn't charged the last time.' Without hesitation, the chap behind the grille said, 'Well, that will be two pounds, then.'

THE must-have invitation for fashionistas in Edinburgh was the official opening party of the city's Armani shop. One guest who sipped wine and looked around the racks was leaving the store when he was handed a heavy Armani gift bag. Coolly waiting until he got into his taxi before looking inside, he was dismayed to see that the goodies in the chic bag consisted only of a book detailing the history of Giorgio's empire. He disgustedly told the taxi driver of his disappointment at the contents when the driver told him, 'Yes, it's been the talk of the drivers tonight. So many of them have picked up folk from the shop, then found the book left in the back of the cab afterwards.'

SMOKING bans in some shops reminded a reader of when the Asda supermarket in Blantyre banned smoking in its cafeteria off the main shopping area. A disgruntled shopper remonstrated with a security guard, telling him, 'How can you ban smoking when you openly sell fags on the premises?' The security guard wisely replied, 'Aye, well, we also sell condoms, but that disnae mean you can . . .'

LISA Paterson of Connecticut was back in Scotland for the New Year when she found herself in the bedlam of the Marks & Spencer

food hall on the last day of the year with a queue like an execution. After waiting a few minutes, she was tapped on the shoulder by the pleasant-looking chap in his 50s behind her, who said, 'Excuse me, missus. Can I go in front of you so that I can rush home and catch my wife with her lover?' A bemused Lisa managed to stammer the reply, 'Why would you want to walk in on that?' when the chap's wife, who was, in fact, standing there, told him, 'You behave yourself.'

A YOUNG chap in an upmarket Glasgow chocolate shop was studying the boxes for so long that an assistant asked if he needed help. The chap explained, 'I must have a box of chocolates that really looks like a swanky box of chocolates for my nan's birthday. Last year, I gave her a hamper from Marks & Spencer – and she told everyone I had given her a box of messages.'

ISHBEL Hurley recalls that when her mum worked in the M&S store in Greenock a while ago, a scruffy youngster came into the shop after the New Year holidays saying his mum had sent him for Jannie Wan biscuits because they were cheap. Assistants searched the shop, but there was no sign of any commodities from the Jannie Wan brand. It was only after further interrogation of the lad that they discovered he had been sent out for biscuits which had gone beyond their sell-by date of January 1.

A READER coming through to Glasgow from Edinburgh by bus on Christmas Eve could not help overhearing the mobile phone conversation of the pretty young girl sitting behind her with her pal. She could hear the girl telling the person down the phone, 'What, a ball? Does he need a ball? I don't know where I can get a ball – the shops will be mobbed.' Our reader could not bear the thought of some youngster not getting a ball for Christmas, and was about to turn round and suggest the girl try John Lewis, across the road from the bus depot, when the girl turned to her pal and muttered, 'A wee ball for the f****** dog . . . I ask you.'

FRANK Inglis of Bishopton was in his local store looking for Parmesan cheese for a recipe. He spotted a tray labelled 'grated cheese' and, picking up a bag, he took it to the checkout, held it up before the girl and asked her what kind of cheese it was. 'Grated,' she replied.

JIM Buchan of Shawlands, Glasgow, tells us about a couple looking for a new bed who were checking out the merchandise in a Glasgow store when they were approached by a young assistant who started showing them divans, wrought-iron beds and futons. Eventually, hubby asked, 'What about pine?' 'No problem,' said the helpful assistant. 'Whitever ye like – cash, cheque, an' we take aw kinds of credit cairds.'

A READER was in his local B&Q plumbing section when he noticed a chap intently reading the instructions on a bottle of drain cleaner. Half an hour later, the guy was still there, poring over the same label. As he works in the building trade, our reader asked if there was a problem. The chap said he was scared the drain cleaner would damage his plastic pipes. Our man told him he needn't worry. 'Why are you so sure?' said the man. Our reader simply pointed at the drain cleaner's container, which was made of plastic.

READER Charles Provan was taken aback when he opened a bottle of normally cheeky claret to find it extremely musty. He took it back to the supermarket in Larkhall where he bought it and explained to the cashier that the wine was 'corked'. To which she replied, 'Aw oor wines are corked, it's only the cheap wans that come screwtapped.'

WHO says Glaswegians aren't inventive? A chap from the city was in a bed store in Paisley buying a couple of mattresses, where staff explained they could not be delivered until the following week. No good for the customer, who wanted them that day. The only thing he could do, staff told him, was go to the warehouse in Patna,

Ayrshire. Later that day, the Paisley staff received a call from Patna. The chap had arrived on a bicycle with two skis strapped to his back. The mattresses were then tied to the skis, and off he peddled back to Glasgow.

TRUSTING souls that we are, we are trying to track down the upmarket delicatessen where a female customer, attempting to make a big impression at a dinner party she was planning, asked if they stocked tinned pigeon. Did the assistant really reply, 'Sorry, madam, no can do.'?

SEVENTEEN

A bit of rough

READERS have fond memories of municipal golf courses where the facilities were not always of the finest. Charlie Mann recalls his first round of golf at Deaconsbank, or Royal Deaky as it is sometimes called, in Glasgow. He had holed out at the first green and began looking for the second tee and green, which was not particularly well marked. When he saw three guys swigging from cans of Tennent's lager making their way to the fifth green, Charlie asked them where the second green was. 'No bother, pal, it's over there,' said the lager drinker, pointing at a green with a red flag. 'But that has a red flag on it, and the first has a yellow,' replied a puzzled Charlie. 'Look, mate,' replied lager man. 'You paid £3.50 to get on here – if you want flags the same colour, f*** off to Gleneagles.' Charlie thanked him for his help.

JIM Young told us of the council-run cricket pitch at Mountblow in Clydebank, overlooked by a squat, heavily boarded pavilion, where he arrived with a team from Clydesdale on Glasgow's south side, who were pleasantly surprised to see a council employee out marking the wicket. As they conveyed their thanks, the chap replied, 'Nae bother, pal,' adding, as he strolled off with brushes

and paint, 'but ah couldnae remember if a cricket pitch was 22 or 24 yairds long so ah just made it 23 – hope that's OK.'

A READER in Newton Mearns told us about his mother-in-law phoning him at five in the morning from Paisley to tell them that she kept hearing a voice saying, 'Hello Valerie,' which persisted even though searches of the flat revealed nothing. He wearily mounted his own investigation and finally discovered her smart smoke detector, which was relaying the electronic message 'Low battery'.

A VIGNETTE from Glasgow's south side, where an angry chap, through the effects of either drink or drugs, was shouting and bawling, offering to fight everyone in sight and kicking out at the windows of parked cars. As worried car-owners called the police, the situation was calmed down by a passer-by who took the chap suffering from his personal demons by the arm, talked to him gently, sat down with him and generally pacified him. When an onlooker praised him for his actions, he told him, 'I work for the housing department. We're used to dealing with people who get in a state.'

PITY the young waiter in the Glasgow West End restaurant who had to deal with a raucous table of four ladies on a night out. Perhaps they were having a private bet on who could give the poor chap a beamer, as when one of the four ordered a steak and was asked how she wanted it cooked, she told him, 'Like my love life.' As he continued to look at her in a puzzled fashion, she finally hooted loudly, 'Very rare!'

LONG-TIME East Kilbride resident Joe McGinty recalled the town once boasting a family of 22, owing to a couple each having seven children from previous marriages and going on to jointly create eight more offspring. The family's patriarch frequently sought refuge by playing the harmonica in local pubs. Legend insists that he was once interrupted by his wife sticking her head round a pub door ordering, 'Come hame, noo! Your kids and my kids are fighting with oor kids.'

AN Ayrshire couple on holiday in the Costa del Sol were amused by the antics of a fellow Scottish couple at the pool. The unsettled wife continually asked her husband to adjust the parasol so that she was always in the shade. No matter how he tilted it, she was unhappy with the result, until finally he scathingly blurted out, 'I know what I'll do – I'll move the sun.'

A MIDDLE-AGED woman confesses to us that she decided to update her underwear drawer by buying a thong. When she tried it on, she thought something wasn't quite right so she called her teenage daughter into the bedroom to get her advice. 'Mum,' said her daughter, 'you've got it on back to front.'

AN English tourist tells us of a trip to Scotland when she accompanied a Japanese couple who were keen to experience the hills and glens of the Highlands. Unfortunately, the Japanese girl had a serious asthma attack. The English girl said she would stay and comfort the stricken visitor while her boyfriend sprinted off to the nearest phone to summon an ambulance. Sadly, when he arrived at a phone box he realised he didn't know the English word for asthma. Which is why the emergency operator was wondering how a chap with a strange accent came to be shouting down the phone, 'Come quick! My girlfriend has very bad breath!' Fortunately, the truth was soon established and all was well.

THIS reminded one emergency operator of the young lady from Glasgow who dialled 999 and asked for the police. The young woman was in quite an agitated state and it took some time to make sense of what she was phoning about. It eventually turned out that she had bought a pair of trousers that did not fit her and she wanted a police escort to go back to the shop with her in case they refused to give her the money back.

NURSES operating the Blood Transfusion Service's mobile donation centres occasionally lament the fact that they're no longer supervised aboard their buses by a doctor. One such practitioner, a starchy and humourless chap, was once somewhat dubious about a potential donor, a wee Glasgow woman. 'Is that herpes?' the doctor asked, studying the woman suspiciously. 'No,' she replied, 'it's a tight perm my daughter gave me.'

APPEARING at the Edinburgh Fringe was *Glory of Gothenburg – The Musical*, which was indeed a musical about three brothers following Aberdeen to their European Cup-Winners' Cup success. In the show, the girlfriend of one of the brothers accuses him of loving Aberdeen Football Club more than her. During the original run in Aberdeen, this immediately brought a shout from a member of the audience of, 'Darling, he loves Rangers more than you.' Which was the best laugh of the night.

TRYING to defend his profession from his sceptical mates' withering scorn in a Glasgow pub the other night, a lawyer was eventually heard to blurt out, 'It's the 99 per cent of lawyers who give the rest of us a bad name.'

FOUR thirsty Glaswegian cyclists touring Ireland entered a shabby, dimly lit Ballymena pub whose sole concession to the twenty-first century was a TV showing some sporting event. Speaking in an impenetrable accent, an elderly habitué started chatting, asking one holidaymaker, 'What d'ye think o' the tans?' Fearing this meant loyalist Ulster's old protectors, the Black and Tans, the visitor sought a neutral path through the sectarian minefield by stammering, 'I've never thought . . . I don't know enough to form an opinion.' The old boy began gesturing exasperatedly at the telly, where Wimbledon was in full swing, crying, 'Tim Henman! The tans! The tans!'

THIS reminded Michael Scanlan of Edinburgh of the time he was in a Cork pub with English friends when one English chap asked a local woman, 'How do you feel about The Cause?' The woman was a bit flustered and replied that it wasn't something she really wanted to talk about and that it was a very delicate subject. Only after some further questioning did folk realise that the Home

Counties toff was merely asking her opinion on the sisters-and-brother combo The Corrs.

DRAMATIST Simon McCallum was inspired to pen his Radio 4 play *The Last Ten* by his love of boxing. A Scotland internationalist in his teens, Simon returned to the ring to record sound effects for his drama at a gym in Partick, Glasgow. 'You've boxed before,' noted one of the gym's regular patrons. 'Aye, but not for ten years,' replied Simon, who gave up boxing to be an actor. He was immediately favoured with a conspiratorial look and the sympathetic words, 'Been inside?'

EIGHTEEN

The anorexic politician

SCOTS have a healthy disregard for their politicians, but occasionally the politicians themselves can tell a good story. Owing to his normal dour demeanour, the chancellor of the exchequer Gordon Brown does not often come across as someone with a store of wisecracks. So we were delighted when a chap in the world of showbiz told us that he was at one of those receptions where the government courts the great and the good of the creative industry, and he got chatting to Gordon. The chatty chancellor told him of the recent G7 meeting, where Jacques Chirac, the French president, was bemoaning in his speech how much the economic climate was adversely affecting France's ability to maintain a competitive edge. At that, George Bush turned to Tony Blair next to him and murmured, 'The trouble with the French is, they don't have the word entrepreneur in their dictionary.'

MSP Tommy Sheridan was invited to play for charity team Dukla Pumpherston at Firhill to raise money for the Scottish Motor Neurone Disease Association. Tommy emailed them to say he would be back from holiday in time to play and ended the email

> **FOUND,** Saturday night in Burra Hall, upper set of false teeth. – Tel.
>
> **LOST** at Burra Hall on Saturday night. Upper set of dentures. If found – Tel.

with 'In Solidarity' in his customary way. The charity thanked him in a return email for his attendance, but added, 'Hope you enjoyed your holiday in Solidarity. Bring the photies when you come on Sunday.'

PLAYWRIGHT Alan Bennett told a story at the Edinburgh Book Festival about a friend who had to show the then Prime Minister Margaret Thatcher around a university where on the walls there were portraits of various university chancellors, including one called Cole. Bearing in mind this was soon after the miners' strike, he deliberately told Mrs Thatcher that the chap's name was Dole. Why? He was hoping that she would read the proper name below the portrait and then, without thinking, utter the words, 'Cole not Dole.'

TONY Blair has been in international hot water for some time now, accused in Europe of too readily committing Britain to George Bush's war on Iraq. This frostiness, though, wasn't in evidence at Tony's first major diplomatic visit to France when, after meeting French premier Lionel Jospin, he declared, 'I like Lionel in many different ways.' A civil servant who was on the trip tells us that this was translated into French as, 'I desire Lionel in many different positions.'

THE ANOREXIC POLITICIAN

A DELEGATE at the Scottish Trades Union Congress's annual conference declared after a speech by a visiting politician, 'My father told me politicians were like bananas – green and straight when they start out, yellow and bent when they finish up.'

SPOTTED at Scottish Opera's Ring Cycle was former Conservative foreign minister Malcolm Rifkind, who bumped into Hugh Kerr, press officer of Tommy Sheridan's Scottish Socialist Party. 'You know, Malcolm,' said Hugh cheerily, 'if you had won Edinburgh Pentlands at the last election, you would be Tory leader today.' Without a pause, Malcolm dramatically wiped his brow and said, 'Whew, that was a close shave.'

SCOTTISH Socialist Rosie Kane's humanitarian gesture of putting up in her home a single mum and her child seeking asylum did not impress everyone. A Tory MSP at the Scottish Parliament was heard telling an unmarried colleague, 'You've been taking single women into your flat for years, and never getting any credit for it.'

A HOLYROOD contact assures us this is an apocryphal tale, not in any way pertaining to leading QC and Labour MSP for Govan, Gordon Jackson: 'A distinctively shaped west of Scotland politician recently entered a top Glasgow tailoring concern, telling an assistant, "I need a new suit. Anything off the peg that will fit me?" Concerned for the tailor's reputation, the reply was, "I very much hope not, sir."'

A CHAP who has a passing acquaintance with the Scottish National Party noticed a few of its MSPs, including former deputy leader Roseanna Cunningham, dining in an Edinburgh tapas bar. Feeling in a benevolent mood, he told the waiter to take them a bottle of wine and put it on his bill. He later asked the waiter what it cost, but was told, 'I don't know yet, sir. They're still voting on whether to have red or white.'

THE grande dame of the Scottish National Party, Winnie Ewing, has retired from the Scottish Parliament, but her wisdom lives on in the book of quotations, *Ultimate Wit*, collated by Des MacHale. Winnie is quoted as saying, 'A chill ran along the Labour back benches looking for a spine to run up.'

SCOTLAND's pharmacists took a stall at the SNP conference and then sent a young woman around delegates offering them free health checks. One mightily sturdy Nat, his waistcoat buttons straining, asked if they could check if he had anorexia. Seeing his girth, the perplexed girl asked dubiously, 'Why do you think you're anorexic?', which was the perfect feed for him to reply, 'Because when I look in the mirror, I think I'm fat.'

WITH panto season approaching, we talked to one writer who was asked to compose a version of *Sleeping Beauty* for South Lanarkshire Council to promote in one of its halls. Alas, the heavy hand of censorship descended and he was told to remove the following gag – Tweedle Dum: 'Come and see Sleeping Beauty.'

Tweedle Daft: 'Has she truly been asleep for 100 years?' Tweedle Dum: 'Aye, she works for South Lanarkshire Cooncil.'

OUR Northern Ireland correspondent told us about old provo, now education minister, Martin McGuinness visiting an integrated primary school in Belfast. Martin was chatting away to the kiddies in best politician manner when he discovered one of the little ones was keen on fishing. So he asked the child what he used for bait. To the delight of the grown-ups standing around, the young chap piped up, 'Sure, we just bate them over the head with a big stick.'

THE former Scottish Nationalist MSP Dorothy-Grace Elder attended a meeting about flood damage in Glasgow's Shettleston and the lack of government funds to help the victims. One woman asked why there was no help, only to be told that it was because it was being treated as an act of God, 'Good Lord,' said the woman, 'they politicians certainly know how to pass the buck.'

NINETEEN

Invite to a bender

A COUPLE were getting ready for a night out. The taxi arrived and the wife got into it while hubby searched the house for the cat to make sure she was kept in the kitchen where she wouldn't do any damage. His wife, meanwhile, was telling the waiting taxi driver that her husband would be there shortly, once he said goodnight to her mother – a harmless ploy to suggest that the house would not be empty. Two minutes later, hubby jumped in the cab and announced a little too loudly, 'Sorry about that. The stupid so-and-so was hiding under the bed, and it took me long enough to poke her out with a coat hanger.'

DESIGNER Victor Brierley of Glasgow was in contact with a client, Carlton Hotels in Amsterdam, when he found himself talking to a new member of staff, a Mona Bender. She was puzzled as to why he was insisting she was perfectly named to attend an office Christmas party in Glasgow.

BOARDING a late-night bus in Argyle Street, Glasgow, on a Saturday, two inebriated couples discovered a winter wonderland of seasonal song as three forty-something women harmonised sweetly

122

on 'Away in a Manger'. The two couples then joined the whole bus in lustily crooning 'The 12 Days of Christmas'. Sadly, discord emerged when the couples reached their destination, Partick. One of the males was so enjoying conducting the impromptu motorised choir and bellowing 'Five gold rings!' that although he had no idea where the bus was going, he announced he was staying aboard. 'Ah'll get a taxi back,' he slurred, before being buffeted about the head and hauled away by his glowering partner.

IS Glasgow truly the capital of twenty-first century gourmet taste it boasts it is? The proprietor of a chic Glasgow restaurant reported an elderly woman recently summonsing him to her table, sternly stating, 'Ah'll huv a capper-sheeno – an' no' too much sheeno, son.'

AN easy mistake to make. At the Brewer's Fayre pub near the old Glasgow Zoo, a chap approached a barmaid and asked, 'Can you tell me where the gents' toilet is, please?' So the harassed barmaid swiftly told him, 'Against the back wall.' After letting that information sink in, he naturally had to ask her, 'Eh, do you not have a small room I could go into?' But her puzzled look suggested that his attempt at humour had gone straight over her head.

FEMALE guests arriving at curry magnate Charan Gill's annual charity dinner, The Hottest Night of the Year, were greeted at Glasgow's Moat House Hotel with a ceremonial Indian bindi to wear on their foreheads. One thoughtful guest knew his mum's pal would arrive late, and so belatedly returned to the check-in desk. 'Can you tell me where the bindis are?' the lad asked, and was advised by the non-Asian receptionist, 'Have you looked at the seating plan?'

WE hear of a Territorial Army training-camp weekend when a sergeant, passing the barracks after lights out, heard a bit of a racket inside. Throwing open the door, he shouted, 'Listen. When

I said "good night", what I really meant was "shut the f*** up".' The room fell silent, and as he turned on his heel, a voice was heard from the darkness: 'Good night, sergeant.'

WORD reaches us of a squaddie from Kilbirnie in Ayrshire whose regiment was involved in the push towards Basra in the Iraq War. En route, they were waved down by an Iraqi lad looking for food and water. The unit gave him what they could spare, but he still made signs that he wanted more water for his family. So the Ayrshire corporal scribbled him a large printed sign to hold up to the next unit that came along. Which is why the following crew found a lone Arab boy in the middle of the desert waving a placard which read, 'Gie's yer water, ya bawbags.'

AN old-fashioned street preacher was giving it laldy in Glasgow's city centre the other day and while brandishing the Bible was telling all and sundry that it was the greatest story ever told. This proved too much for a chap with just a suspicion of drink who turned and told the preacher, 'Naw. Gremlins. Christmas time. Little cute furry creatures as presents who turn into monsters when they get wet. The whole place devastated. Now that was the greatest story ever told,' before walking on and leaving the Bible-thumper, for once, lost for words.

A UNION official in Glasgow tells us of her conference which had the entirely laudable intention of ensuring that all delegates could work free from sexual harassment. She explained, 'The powers-that-be set up a service for people who might feel that they were being harassed so that they could be counselled and given assistance to sort it out. However, these good intentions were somewhat diminished when those of us who had offered to help with it found the name on the door of the room that had been made available to us – the Sexual Harassment Action Group. Needless to say, we were all known as the Shag Patrol from then on.'

YES, the charitable warmth of Glaswegians at Christmas time. A young woman was using one of the city-centre car parks and had entered the lift to return to her car, when the lift stuck. The door hadn't completely closed and through the slight gap she could see another woman approaching. 'The lift's stuck,' shouted the girl through the gap. The approaching woman thought about this for a moment before telling her, 'Oh, I'll just use the stairs then,' and walking off. The trapped girl did eventually get out and is beginning to see the funny side.

LARGS couple John and Pat Parr took in a golden Labrador which had been trained to the gun in Ayrshire but didn't make the grade as a gundog and was becoming a family pet instead. The only problem was that anything it picked up in the house it would never drop. Eventually, their daughter contacted the gamekeeper who had trained the dog so that she was able to tell her parents that the trick was to tell him to sit, put your hand under his mouth and say, 'Dead!', at which point he would drop whatever he was clutching in his jaws. Alas, this did not work at first, but after a few days her dad phoned her to announce success. Pondering over the problem, and realising the dog was trained in Ayrshire, he simply changed the command to 'Deid!' and it worked every time.

CHRIS Rafferty tells us of being out celebrating the early retirement of a colleague. When they approached an Edinburgh west end bar, the doorman told the chap, 'You can't get in, sir, you're staggering.' His reply to the steward of, 'You're no' bad lookin' yerself – but why should that stop me gettin' in?' failed to win him ingress.

WHAT about Superman taking Batman for a wee fly about, but Batman being disappointed as low cloud spoiled the view. Superman reaches down and says, 'We're over New York.' 'How do you know?' asks Batman. 'I've just touched the top of the Empire State Building,' says Superman. Shortly afterwards, Superman reaches down again through the cloud and declares they are over Paris – because he can feel the top of the Eiffel Tower. Later, he reaches down again and states they're now over Glasgow. 'How do you know?' Batman says for a third time. 'Because,' Superman replies, 'someone's nicked my watch.'

WE are assured this is a genuine transcript of a Glasgow 999 call.

Operator: 'Hello. How can we help?'

Woman: 'Ah'm ower nine months' pregnant, an' ma waters huv jist broke.'

Operator: 'OK, calm down. First, I need to know where you're ringing from.'

Woman: 'Fae the waist doon, hen.'

TWENTY

Neds

NEDS: whey-faced skinny guys in white tracksuits and Burberry baseball caps – now isn't that a disaster for a smart fashion label? – drinking Buckfast and always hurrying through town even though they really have nowhere to go, while they turn round and curse and swear at their gold-wearing burger-munching girlfriends bringing up the rear – and what large rears they have. It is easy to make fun of neds – the name possibly deriving from 'non-educated delinquents'. But on balance we refer to Cloudo, the pseudonym of student-press award-winner Shaun Murphy of Glasgow University who writes a column as Cloudo putting the life of the ned in perspective. We quote from Cloudo attending a Student Representative Council meeting at Glasgow Uni and crossing swords with a student activist. 'Here mate who dyeh say yer fightin?' 'The class war, man.' 'Whit? Heremate, talkin rubbish at meetins aw day doesn'y get anything done, n neither dis makin crap banners n hingin thum oot yer winday by the way. See if yez want tae fight come doon tae ma bit thirs folk fightin every night way bottles n knifes, no sittin in the QMU havin a meetin tae organise a meetin, na'am sayin?' 'Em, it's called raising awareness, and we're fighting these battles on fees for people like you, man.' 'Youse urny fightin nothin fir me, your jist a cheapskate n don't want tae pay fir yer uni lifestyle. A get taxed 40 bucks a week tae keep clowns like you here, a dinny see you payin yir council tax ya mad rocket. Aye boost about n 'raise awareness' aww yis want bit enda the day the only hing your fightin tae improve is yer ain CV.' And so the division between neds and students in Glasgow goes on.

TWO young mothers from the Mearns are in a Giffnock coffee shop discussing trips with their children. 'I'm taking my two youngest to Pollok House at Hallowe'en for a ghost walk that's been organised.' Her friend asks what it consists of, so she hazards a guess: 'Oh, I expect they just pay some locals to jump out of the bushes in a threatening manner.' 'So, no change there, then,' muses her friend.

THE well-dressed chap in the bar of the Tron Theatre was perhaps just a tad too loud as he told his drinking companion, 'What do you hear when you hold a shellsuit to your ear?' He then answered his question himself: 'Paisley.'

JIM Buchan was walking through the St Enoch Centre in Glasgow when his attention was arrested by two men with good-looking birds on their arms – feathered ones. A company from Perthshire was trying to encourage shoppers to buy a day-long falconry course. A sizeable crowd of punters gathered around one especially magnificent 2 ft-tall bird of prey as it perched impassively on the falconer's leather glove. It was then Jim heard a callow Glaswegian youth observe to his pal, 'Haw, man, check oot that pure mad craw thing.'

A NEW take on begging is observed in Glasgow's George Square. A young man crossing the square is hailed by a mendicant on one of the benches who asks if he would like to 'sponsor a pigeon'. Curious, the chap asks how much it would be to sponsor such a bird. 'Twenty pence,' he is told, 'but they always fly aboot in fives.'

BROADCASTER Stephen Jardine was presenting telly news programme *Scotland Today* live from Edinburgh when, to show the jollity of the streets, he asked the cameraman to pan across to a cheery chap stripped to his waist supping a beer. The can-carrying chap seemed a bit perturbed, and afterwards he went up to Stephen to ask if that had been a live broadcast. When Stephen confirmed it was, the chap's face fell and he declared, 'I'm on the run.' He then added, 'Still, at least ma maw might have seen me,' before slipping back into the crowd.

FORMER Glasgow resident Norman McLeod, now living in London, was waiting for a bus at Waterloo when he heard a young lady with a posh Glasgow accent. She was chatting to her boyfriend when a mendicant, who had also heard the Scottish voices, approached the couple and asked if they could spare a 'fellow Jock' some change. The boyfriend, though, went further than that and nipped into a fast-food store behind them, emerging with chips and a burger for the shabby old chap. And the very observant Norman claims that as the dosser walked off, the woman told her boyfriend, 'I don't know, Donald, that junk food must play havoc with his cholesterol.'

A READER from Shawlands was walking past the jobcentre in Glasgow's Battlefield Road when he noticed that a number of its windows had been boarded up after some wanton vandalism. He reckons there must have been about ten shattering blows dealt to the windows for some reason. Then he noticed some wag had stuck a small note in a corner on which was scrawled, 'Glazier wanted. Apply within.'

A GROUP of Glasgow girls were having a drink when they were joined by some likely lads who attempted to chat them up. Eventually, the girls stood up to leave, announcing they had to go to a concert. At that, one of the chaps lifted his trouser-leg from his ankle to reveal an electronic tag and declared, 'It's OK. Ah've got to be home for nine anyway.'

EVIDENCE that young people are ready to embrace the Scottish Executive's recent moves to combat child obesity and improve their fitness. Puffing and panting, a ten-year-old boy was scurrying painfully along Union Street, Glasgow, under the weight of a full crate of Coca-Cola. As he was heard asserting to a companion, 'That's the last time ah'm knockin' wan o' these.'

DURING a heated family discussion about business morality, the elderly head of a respected Italian–Glaswegian fast-food dynasty confessed to his most shameful retail initiative. It came one night forty years ago after he'd opened his mobile chip shop on its customary pitch in gang-riven Govan. A breathless young man ran up, urgently requesting a bottle of ginger. When asked what flavour he required, the youth pointed over his shoulder, replying, 'It disnae matter! It's only tae hit *him* ower the heid wi'!' Il padrone ruefully admitted to joy at shifting one of his less popular soft drinks: dandelion and burdock.

THE goths who hang around Glasgow's Gallery of Modern Art are charming people, as we have pointed out before, though slightly alarming if you don't know them. One chap walking past the other night tells us: 'One young lad had a particularly doom-laden T-shirt with "I Hate the World and I Want to Die" written across it. I then heard him telling his mate, "I don't think my mum will let me."'

TWENTY-ONE

Scotland's money pit

IF there is one thing that Scots enjoy, it is a good moan. So when the cost of the Scottish Parliament rose quicker than a plumber's estimate, the new building was talked about everywhere – including, of course, in the columns of The Diary. When Sean Connery, arguably Scotland's most famous actor, made a short film about the building of the Scottish Parliament, the Parliament's broadcasting unit enthusiastically invited all the MSPs to see the five-minute film. Immediately, one MSP declared, 'Apparently it's called *007: A Licence to Print Money*.'

IT seems our MSPs are belatedly trying to raise cash for the Holyrood building. The Scottish Parliament's website has launched an online shop with the politicians very much in mind. For £15, they can buy the book *High Impact Speeches: How to Create and Deliver Words That Move Minds*. Obviously, not many have forked out for it so far. But when they want to unwind after a hard day legislating, they can buy a large hip-flask, or a Scottish Parliament corkscrew at £22.50. A bit steep, perhaps, but, as the shop says, it is a 'very elegant matt-and-chrome combined corkscrew and bottle-opener engraved with the Scottish

Parliament logo'. In addition, there is a Scottish Parliament jigsaw, which presumably works on the basis that you throw the pieces in the air and wherever they fall you try to make some sense out of it – or are we getting confused with the plans for the Holyrood building? But hurry. There is no guarantee all these prices won't double over the next few weeks.

HOLYROOD researchers often text MSPs with last-minute information during debates. One female MSP was recently in full rhetorical flow when she became more than a little disconcerted by an urgent text message that, she eventually divined, was intended for a male colleague. The message? 'Your flies are open.'

AN Edinburgh Council environmental project asked Dumbiedykes' P7s to design a better future for their somewhat disadvantaged inner-city scheme. A film crew recorded the process, which involved the budding social architects poring over a detailed scale model of Dumbiedykes and its immediate environs. Naturally, the model included a life-like polystyrene representation of the housing scheme's emergent new neighbour –

Holyrood. The film-makers later spotted a yellow Post-it note stuck to Holyrood's side, bearing one young Dumbiedyker's two-word ideal town plan: 'No parliament.'

A READER traipsing round a Wimpey housing development in first minister Jack McConnell's Lanarkshire constituency was surprised to see one of the house styles was called The Holyrood – a snip at £153,000. He could not resist, of course, telling the sales lady, 'No thanks. It would just be throwing good money after bad, the cost would go up and up, and we'd have no idea when we'd be able to move in.'

FRIENDS can be so cruel when you need their support most. A chap in Tillicoultry was in his local explaining that he had split up with his wife – and to make matters worse, she had kept the satellite dish. Within minutes, the Volunteer Arms was resounding to the sound of his pals singing their version of the Bob Marley classic – 'No Woman, No Sky'.

WE will spare the name of the west of Scotland mother-in-law who was looking after the grandchildren while their mother was working and took in a delivery of a bouquet of flowers. When her daughter-in-law arrived home, the mum-in-law told her, 'Lovely flowers came from Lily, Pauline, May and Stan.' The puzzled mum, not recognising the names, went into the kitchen, opened the card with them and realised her mistake. She went back to the living room and announced, 'I wish you would wear your specs before reading the warning, Mum – it says lily pollen may stain.'

ALWAYS good to see Scots doing well in international competitions – such as in Nimbin, a small settlement in Australia's New South Wales, famous for its alternative lifestyles and annual 'mardi grass festival' which attracts thousands campaigning for the legalisation of cannabis. The most recent festival included events such as the quickest to roll a joint – and, yes, it was won by a backpacker from Castlemilk. Our exile in Australia, Gary Johnston, met the winner, of whom he says, 'Big Peasy from Castlemilk said his skills had been honed on Croftfoot golf course where he once skinned up while sheltering under an umbrella in a force-four gale, to the astonishment and admiration of his mates.' His nomination for Scottish Sports Personality of the Year is surely not far away.

ÉMIGRÉ Glaswegian Bill Dunlop is transfixed by a radio advertising campaign in Washington DC. It's for the Salvation Army, with the slogan: 'Down the road, it'll do some good.' The Sally Army is calling upon affluent Americans to donate any unused items – particularly old cars. The ad outlines the benefits accruing to generous car donors: 'You'll be saved the trouble of selling it. You'll get a tax credit. You'll feel really good about it – except when you're standing at the bus stop.'

A SCOT now resident in London has spotted a 'pure swanky' silver BMW being driven around Putney by someone our informant is certain is a fellow Celt. The giveaway is the motor's personalised number plate. Surely only a Glaswegian would openly boast of being an EDJ 1T.

SETTING out from Spain on a brief trip home, another Scottish expat was ordered to 'get some euros just in case' from Malaga airport's cash machine. He returned to his wife empty-handed, saying the machine's screen display offered to conduct the transaction in several languages – Spanish, French, German, Italian – but not English. His wife was baffled, but refrained from comment until the couple were close to touchdown in Glasgow when she turned to him, asking, 'That on-screen display you read, specifying Spanish, French, German, Italian – what language was it in?' She was unsurprised by her man's blithe reply: 'English.'

> **MISSING DUNBEG** area, very friendly neutered tabby boy. Telephone Pat, Argyll Animal Aid

TYPOGRAPHICAL errors we have loved. Dave Cook of Motherwell treasures an old *Edinburgh Evening News* Saturday-night football special. Reporting on a game at Central Park, Cowdenbeath, it asserted that the home team had been awarded a penalty after one of their players 'was unfairly tickled in the box'.

SCOTTISH Television's Glasgow newsroom laid on a swanky stretch limo to transport the ageless Joan Collins – estimated by carbon-dating to be 70 – from the King's Theatre, where she was starring in a play, for an interview in the station's studios. Backroom staff marvelled at Joan's elaborate coiffure, her extravagantly stylish garb and the painstaking detail of her facial make-up. This contrasted oddly with Joan's pithy verdict on the limo: 'Too ostentatious.'

MIKE Blair of Rothesay was on a sales mission to America with ferry company CalMac when his business flight from Tampa landed at Washington with lots of suit-wearing laptop warriors jumping up trying to get off the plane first. The head stewardess tried to calm them all by announcing, 'In the history of USAir, no passenger has ever reached the gate before the aircraft.' Such irony, though, was lost on the American businessmen, who still pressed forward. So she then announced: 'A camera will descend from the overhead bins and take pictures of all passengers not seated. USAir will release these pictures to all airlines, thus guaranteeing you crap service thereafter.' And the suits all sat down.

IRASCIBLE *Daily Record* sports legend Alex Cameron may be gone, but he's not easily forgotten. Chiefy, as Alex was known, was once in Leeds at a Celtic–Leeds United encounter. Directly in front of the press box, an excitable chap wearing a tweed deerstalker kept standing up and spoiling Chiefy's view, soon being told, 'Sit f****** down!' At this, the fellow turned round and jovially growled, 'Hello, Alex. Shtill doing *Shportsh Schene*?' Chiefy turned to his journalistic colleagues and, bearing a look of genuine puzzlement, asked, 'Who the f*** is that?' It's a good job 007 is thick skinned.

VETERAN football broadcaster Archie Macpherson is regarded with much affection by armchair viewers. A football website cites a number of gems from his long career, including:

- I predicted in August that Celtic would reach the final. On the eve of that final, I stand by that prediction.
- That's the kind he usually knocks in in his sleep – with his eyes closed.
- And then there was Johan Cruyff, who, at 35, has added a whole new meaning to the word *anno domini*.

SPEAKING of football, we pass on the remark by one football fan overheard in the pub the other day describing Christian Dailly's performance for Scotland against New Zealand as being 'like a fish out of batter'.

TWENTY-TWO

Cracking the postcode

FOR many folk, the only place to stay in Glasgow was the West End but with house prices rising, just a hint of pretentiousness crept in as the postcode G12 became increasingly desirable to those who worry about such things. The Diary first chronicled the changing tide some time ago when we told of the West End chap stung by a wasp in his garden and shouting through to his wife in the kitchen for vinegar to pour on it. Her reply of 'Balsamic or ordinary?' began our quest for G12 stories.

WEST END style-bar Bloody Mary's had to change the name over its door because of a trademark dispute. And with the metal letters already bought, the owners wanted to merely rearrange them. Diary readers were up to the challenge. Showing some perspicacity about the West End, Joe Mullen suggested Arsold My Boy. Angus Johnston rather ungentlemanly proffered My Lady Boors, while Jim Campbell went for the more prosaic My Bloody Ars – sadly a letter missing there, Jim. But, for sheer inspired daftness, we commend Stuart McMillan, out in Hong Kong, who said, 'It seems to me that the West End could do with a few more pubs that appeal to a wider clientele and are therefore upmarket,

ethnically themed, and gay friendly. So I would suggest that Mr O'Ladyboys would attract the desired crowd.'

HYNDLAND Secondary headmaster Ian Alexander fights long and hard against pretentious G12 stereotypes, forever pointing out that his school roll encompasses all social classes. However, Ian recently told colleagues of the time two female pupils approached him in a state of great distress. 'Sir, sir, it's the man in the corner shop!' they shrieked, causing Ian to experience a frisson of dread. 'He's selling Crunchies past their sell-by date.'

FURTHER proof – not that it's needed – of G12's cruel ambivalence towards local celebrities. Lisa Melvin tells Pat Byrne's West End website that she spotted Belle and Sebastian's Stuart Murdoch, stating, 'Can't get away from him. Not only do I see him on Byres Road, in Tinderbox and in the Woodside all the time, he did a great injustice and turned up at my flatmate's birthday party the other week. Quite odd that someone even vaguely famous has nothing better to do on a Friday night than turn up randomly at rubbish student parties, but there you have it.'

THE things you hear in Glasgow's West End . . . a couple were enjoying their meal in a G12 restaurant when the rather flamboyant male gestured for the waitress to come over. 'Could you ask the chef,' he said in a slightly too-loud voice, 'whether he prefers boys or girls?' As the waitress tried to fathom out the request, the diner added, 'Because the paella was so good, one of us will have to sleep with him.'

TWO G12 women of a certain age recently met in a West End coffee shop. 'Melanie!' one gushed, before continuing, 'I haven't seen you for ages! In fact, the last time I saw you, I swear you had grey hair!' A terrible silence ensued, after which the woman added, 'Did I say that rather too loud?'

A DAFT joke from Glasgow's G12, where the search for reasonably priced tradesmen is now an obsession. A surgeon in the West End discovers his central heating has broken down and, with a chilly weekend beckoning, calls out a plumber in the evening. With the heating fixed, he is handed a bill for £90 plus VAT. The surgeon explodes, telling the plumber, 'More than £100? It only took you 20 minutes. That's an hourly rate of more than £300. I'm a brain surgeon and don't earn anything like that.' 'I know,' said the plumber sympathetically. 'It was the same when I was a brain surgeon.'

OVERHEARD recently in a West End cafeteria, wherein two G12 matrons were perusing newspaper photographs of some Glasgow charity premiere or other that had been patronised by sundry local D-list celebs. As one woman acidly remarked, 'It's a veritable *Who's That?* of Scottish stage and screen.'

WEDDING etiquette can be a bit strained these days when the father of the bride attends with his new, younger partner. We overheard a G12 mother-of-the-bride in Glasgow's West End telling her pal that she had bought a splendid Armani suit for her daughter's wedding. 'Are you not worried in case your ex's new partner wears something similar?' her friend asked anxiously. 'No,' the mother replied triumphantly. 'I checked with Armani. It doesn't go up to that size.'

A BRIGHT young thing in Glasgow's G12 was overheard telling a friend that she worked for a major international aid agency, but she had been doing it for a while and it didn't seem to offer any new challenges. 'What?' said her baffled friend. 'Have you eradicated world hunger?'

A GLASGOW G12 woman with just a few more lines on her face than she would really like was meeting a girlfriend for a drink. Her friend arrived, looked at her anxiously and said, 'Did you not go ahead with the cosmetic surgery then?' 'No,' said her pal, taking a swift swig of her Pinot Grigio. 'I chickened out when I saw the surgeon's office was full of portraits by Picasso.'

A G12 lady of the blue-rinsed variety suffered a fire in her kitchen at home. When asked if it was the chip pan that had gone up, she indignantly replied, 'Certainly not, I was flambéing courgettes.'

READER Graeme Thomson avers there is a wall in the West End where someone had originally written 'F*** the IRA', but this had been altered by a second hand to read 'F*** the SHIRAZ, drink Merlot.'

AN actress sipping her wine at a pavement café in Glasgow's West End announced to her friends around the table that she was a member of the small but select NDT club. When a non-actor enquired what that was, the actress replied, 'Never Done *Taggart*, darling.'

TWENTY-THREE

Nothing like a dame

GLASGOW has always been known as pantomime city, and, no, it has nothing to do with the workings of the local council. Both the King's and Pavilion theatres now take in over a million pounds each at the box office every Christmas. At the Pavilion, manager Ian Gordon remembers a 'Singing in the Rain' number in the pantomime after which one of the dancers came off saying it had been a triumph, as members of the audience were putting their umbrellas up mimicking the actions of the dancers. It was then Ian realised that the roof needed repairing. And former *Coronation Street* glamourpuss Amanda Barrie made her first stage appearance in Glasgow in pantomime. Her landlady, she recalls, had so many children that she shuffled them around and put them in the actors' beds when they were out performing. 'When we returned, worn out after two shows, the children would have wet the beds,' she still remembers, many years later.

AUDIENCE participation is what makes panto so special for actors. One ice queen was rendered immobile by five bulky weans leaping on her costume's long train. She needed freeing by usherettes, undoing her aura of evil majesty. Fife panto audiences are even harder to please. One Saturday-night crowd for *Cinderella* at Dunfermline's Carnegie Hall forsook normal panto convention by throwing the Quality Street back at the performers when the sweeties were cast into the audience. In addition, when Buttons intoned his heartfelt soliloquy of unrequited love for Cinderella, the spell was slightly broken by a lady in the front row shouting out, 'I'd shag ye, Buttons.' Still, it must have been a good show as the leader of a Brownie pack in the audience was heard telling a colleague while leaving, 'Ah laughed so hard ah had to take ma teeth oot fur fear of swallowing them.'

AH, the changing face of youthful humour. A large group of Scouts were visiting a Glasgow panto when one of the leaders took a packet of sweets from one of the boys, telling him off for sneakily buying them on the way back from the toilet when he'd been told not to. The leader then cheerily shared the sweets out among the other helpers only for the wee boy to stand up, point accusingly at him and shout 'child abuse', much to the horror of the rest of the audience. But it did get him his sweets back.

KIRKWALL Grammar School pupils staged a production of the Peter Maxwell Davies opera *The Two Fiddlers* for Orkney's St Magnus Festival. Interviewed by BBC Radio Orkney about his part, one young cast member stated, 'Ah'm part o' a crowd near the end that his tae act posh.' Intrigued, the interviewer asked how he'd gone about acting posh. 'Och, you know,' said the young thespian, 'you jist stand aroond listenin' tae music.'

RETIRED police officer Andy Collins recalls visiting a well-known felon in Greenock's Gibbshill, looking for stolen goods. As Andy was getting the usual denials from the chap, Andy's colleague was bent over the old lag's budgie cage, with his ear beside the budgie, while he loudly declared, 'The stuff is where?' and 'Who brought it?' before ending with an 'OK, that's great, thanks,' as he stood up straight. The perturbed felon, apparently taken in by this charade, leapt over to the cage and shouted at his budgie, 'You shut yir gub or ah'll wring yir neck. Tell them nuthin'.'

HOLIDAYING in Italy, a reader was pleased when a local restaurant owner showered her with praise when she made a fair attempt at using the Italian language course she'd undertaken at home. The beaming Italian told her, 'You speak two languages, you bilingual. You speak many languages, you polyglot. You speak one language, you British.'

READER Paul Lyons was outside Glasgow's Central Station as a Marks & Spencer lorry unloaded metal cages full of milk cartons. One of the cages tipped awkwardly forward, with cartons falling out and bursting on the pavement. At that, a wee Glesca chap walking past didn't even break stride as he bellowed at the driver, 'There's nae point greetin' ower that,' before carrying on his merry way.

SITTING in a long, slow-moving queue of cabs at Queen Street Station, a Glasgow taxi driver feared the worst: a short hire and a swift return to the same long, slow-moving queue. Eventually, three hearty outdoor types in walking gear climbed into his black hack. The cab driver's heart sank when the trio stated their destination – Central Station. The cabbie adopted a neutral tone as he asked his passengers if they'd been away hillwalking. 'The West Highland Way,' they replied proudly. 'The West Highland Way, is it?' said the cabbie. 'Well, a couple hundred more yards won't hurt you then – beat it out of my taxi.'

TRICKY things, Christmas presents. An Edinburgh lady opened a wrapped prezzie to discover what appeared to be a small bottle of champagne, which she popped in the fridge. It was, alas, a bottle of shampoo tricked out like a champagne bottle. But then, if you don't wear your glasses when you open your presents, you aren't going to know that, are you? And a teacher on her way out the door to go to a Christmas party suddenly realised she had no present for the hostess. Grabbing a wrapped object, she threw it to her startled partner and said, 'Check the wrapping. It doesn't say "To Miss McAdam, from Liam, Primary 4" anywhere on it, does it?'

READER Andrew Smith experienced difficulties with the Virgin Trains website, being sent an email stating: 'Unfortunately, as a result of extreme weather conditions recently, we are receiving an unprecedented amount of mail and our response may be delayed.' Andrew was heartened to see the old train excuses being efficiently transferred to the electronic age.

AUNT Betty, aged 74, listened attentively as her niece told her about a couple – teachers who'd taken early retirement – going off to Pakistan and teaching in a missionary school. They came home for a visit before their impending move to India, Aunt Betty's niece continued, where the husband was going to be a church pastor. When Aunt Betty was eventually introduced to the couple, she told the husband, 'It's marvellous you're blessed with so many talents – Asian languages, teaching and having served your time as a plasterer.'

A GLASGOW builder of the old school was dismayed by the terminology employed by a younger tradesman whose work was generally confined to one of Glasgow's more genteel suburban townships, Newton Mearns. Having grown accustomed to measurements being recorded in crude and pithy language, the veteran was appalled one day to hear his contemporary sidekick observe, 'I think I'm just out by a butterfly's wing.'

WIDOWED for some time, a 75-year-old Ayrshire woman imagined she was being tactful when she informed her grown-up daughter about the changes wrought by her romantic involvement with a near-neighbour of a similar age. 'You know, dear,' the elderly woman began in an observation which caused her daughter grave distress, 'when I go to bed these days, I don't take my teeth out.'

A READER tells us his exasperated teenage daughter was turning the living room upside down looking for her mobile phone, until she finally blurted out, 'You would think someone would invent a phone that was stuck to the wall, so you wouldn't lose it.'

NOTHING LIKE A DAME

A CHAP in Glasgow's Nuffield Hospital for a knee operation found his ears under painful attack from a female patient who had decided to chat for Britain about her many ailments. When she proudly stated that it was her fourth hip operation, he asked with a straight face, 'So what are you, then? A centipede?'

PAUL McGivern was once very early for an interview at a business on Edinburgh's outskirts, so he decided to pop into a pub for lunch. Perusing the menu, he noticed that food was available from noon, and it was only quarter to twelve, so he asked the barman if he could order now, or whether he needed to wait. 'No, just order now, sir,' said the barman. 'The chef will only be standing about the kitchen with his finger up his arse.' Commendably, Paul refrained from voicing his order in an all-too-obvious manner: 'If he washes his hands, could I have a sirloin steak?'

AUTHOR Graham Ogilvy was delighted when his home town, Dundee, acquired a decent second-hand bookshop. When he entered its Exchange Street premises, he couldn't resist checking whether his own local history work, *Dundee: A Voyage of Discovery*, was there. There were indeed two copies of the book: a signed copy at £6.50 . . . and an unsigned one for £8.

A JAPANESE visitor arrived at a Glasgow guest house and, after much respectful bowing and hand-shaking, the owner began ushering her guest towards his room. Out of the corner of one eye, however, she spotted her pet dog slinking into the kitchen. She turned on the pooch, pointing imperiously and bellowing in a commanding voice, 'Downstairs!' She then continued towards the guest's room, turning back to him – and finding he wasn't there. He was, of course, downstairs, respectfully awaiting further orders – unlike the dog, which had doubled back to the kitchen and eaten four kippers.

TWENTY-FOUR

Child's play

FATHERS and children – we have put them both in this chapter as they share so many childlike characteristics. It is perhaps best summed up by the story of the three-year-old boy examining his private parts in the bath as his mum was giving him a wash. He eventually said to her, 'Are these my brains?' As she swished the water around him, she replied, 'No, not yet, son.'

GLASWEGIAN exile Stephen Clark was reminded of good, old-fashioned, west of Scotland parenting when he returned to the city and boarded a bus, where a little boy left his mother and determinedly sat at the front of the bus while she was at the back. Continued cries from her that he should join her were ignored by the tot, until she held up a green, stuffed toy and threatened, 'C'mere – or the Teletubby gets it.'

A PARENT was overseeing the eating arrangements for the big family meal on Christmas Day. Due to pressure of numbers, all the adults were in the dining room while all the children were eating next door at the kitchen table. She was buzzing between the two rooms when she heard one of the youngsters tell a cousin, 'I'm getting to eat Christmas dinner in the dining room when one of the old ones dies.'

JIM McCreadie of Mount Vernon tells us of his dad's clashes with Jim's younger sister over what she was doing with her spare time. His authority was rather undermined, however, when he thundered at her, 'Look, don't lie. Do you think I'm as plank as two short thicks?'

JOHN Bruce of Lanarkshire was pitching in to get the family ready for their holidays by farming out his daughter's pets to various neighbours to look after. Says John: 'I duly volunteered to take the goldfish in its tank across the road. The tank had no lid and it was raining. My daughter asked why the neighbour was laughing when I handed the tank to her. I said I didn't know but we eventually found out it was because I had said to her I had covered the tank with a tea towel on the way over to stop the fish getting wet.'

WE are told of a married chap who was exasperating his wife by always having his mobile telephone on at home and disturbing the evening taking calls about work. So, one evening, he pledged to keep the phone off, but surreptitiously kept it on vibrate just in case there was an important call. All was going well until he was perched on the edge of his daughter's bed reading her a bedtime story, when, sure enough, the phone vibrated. Unfortunately, his young daughter shouted out, 'Mum, Dad has just farted on my bed!' When his shocked wife came into the room and asked how he could do something so gross, he was left with the dilemma of trying to work out which answer was going to give him the least grief with his wife.

A YOUNGSTER, not even four, is being looked after in Aberdeenshire by his great aunt and uncle when, during the news on the telly reporting on Blair and Bush's warmongering, the little one pipes up: 'With great power comes great responsibility.' The doting relatives report back to the lad's mum that she has a genius on her

hands, or perhaps even the Grampian equivalent of the Dalai Lama has been found. She sadly has to let them down gently by explaining it is a line from his *Spiderman* video which he constantly watches.

CHILDREN'S author Harry Horse was appearing at the Edinburgh Book Festival and had just begun reading from one of his books when a four-year-old girl in the front row began bawling loudly and inconsolably. Harry soon called a halt, bending down and asking the child's parents what was wrong. The parent told him, 'She's disappointed you're not a horse.'

WE hear of a little lad in Ayrshire who was taken to see the *Nemo* animated film by his mum and who turned round and said to her halfway through, 'You wouldn't want to miss any of this film by going to the toilet, would you?' In a rather distracted way, his mother agreed with him. Which allowed him to tell her, 'So you won't be angry that I've wet my pants?'

THE Scottish charity SCIAF started a Real Gifts campaign which allowed folk to buy a gift such as a pig for a deserving family abroad in return for a certificate explaining what a difference the gift would make. The campaign was extremely popular, but there was a little confusion. One Airdrie family clubbed together to buy a house for a family in Ethiopia for £276. As they explained to their four-year-old niece what they'd done, she grew increasingly excited. Obviously, the gift was a wonderful present but they couldn't help but feel she was a little too enthusiastic. All became clear when she was heard saying Aunty had bought a new holiday home.

AS ithers see us . . . Welshman Dilwyn Phillips has published a little book entitled *Celtic Jokes* – the hard 'c', not the soft 'c' footballing variety. It tells us: 'Little Hamish came home from school and told his mother he had a part in the school play. "Wonderful," says the mother. "What part is it?" "I play the role of the Scottish husband." The mother scowls and says, "Go back and tell your teacher you want a speaking part."'

A GLASGOW businessman tells us he was in town meeting his student daughter, who steered him towards a bookshop where she wanted 'just a couple of books' for her course. A few minutes later, he was back out on the street £150 lighter. Later, his daughter texted him on his mobile phone to thank him for the transaction. The text message read, 'Thanks for the books – but you're still getting put in a nursing home.'

A SCOTTISH grandfather was listening to his student grandchildren enthusiastically explain their plans for taking a year out from their studies and going to Australia, Thailand and other such locations. Eventually, he told them, 'The only time I had a year out from working here in Scotland, Germans were shooting at me.'

CHRIS Thomson tells us of his father-in-law, Graham Hill, and his wife enjoying a quiet whisky at home in Killearn when suddenly there was a power cut. Unable to find any candles, the pair decided to make the most of the romantic interlude, so Graham stumbled in the dark to the kitchen to top up their whiskies. After fumbling around for the Grouse bottle and the ice, he made his way back to the sitting room. Ten minutes later, the lights came back on to reveal the couple romantically sipping from large glasses of whisky with frozen king prawns floating in them.

THE Citizens' Theatre pantomime *Snow White* was weaving its magical spell over innocent Glaswegian children. Having been dragged into the forest by the murderous Huntsman, Snow White found herself abandoned to the deadly attentions of the wild creatures of the woodland. Anxious and frightened, she looked about her in the darkness of the Citz and softly asked, 'What will I do?' A young lady in the audience knew exactly, shouting out, 'I should bloody well run.'

A CONCERNED couple were trying to console their young daughter, who was bereft at the death of her pet hamster. In desperation, her mother told her, 'You know, he's probably up in heaven right now, having a great time with God.' Her tearful daughter exclaimed, 'What would God want with a dead hamster?'

IN A feature titled Walk this Way (Monday, May 24) we implied that, before he became a serious climber, Gordon Sneddon...couldn't tell a Munro from a mountain and thought a crampon was a feminine hygiene product.

This is inaccurate, we apologise for any embarrassment caused.

CHILD'S PLAY

WE are told about the Sunday-school teacher who was trying to get the point across about Jesus still being in everyone's lives and asked the question, 'Where is Jesus today?' Among replies of 'heaven' and so on, one little lad blurted out, 'He's in our bathroom.' Naturally, the teacher asked how was that, so the lad replied, 'Every morning my dad bangs on the bathroom door and yells, "Jesus Christ, are you still in there?"'

TWENTY-FIVE

So I told the doctor . . .

GLASGOW is frequently referred to as 'the sick man of Europe' as its citizens cope with a poor diet, the fags, the booze, the weather and poor housing. So who can blame them for trying to smile through the pain? We commend, for example, the chap giving a pint at the Blood Transfusion Service who had obviously stored away in the recesses of his mind an old joke from the music hall just waiting for the right moment. When he settled in the big, relaxing reclining chair with the tube in his arm, the nurse asked him: 'Comfy?' Who can blame him for replying, 'Govan.'

A MEMBER of staff at Stobhill Hospital was chatting to her regular bus driver about her day and mentioned that a wee deer ran down from behind the mental-health unit onto the road and back again in panic. She said that she phoned security, who said it happens a lot, and the best thing to do was let them run around and hope they find their way home. If you chase them, she continued, their hearts can give out through fright and they can smash themselves into trees and fences in terror. The driver said it was terrible, and that it didn't seem right that they were left to run around. Touched by his concern, she remarked that she didn't realise he was such an animal lover. It was then the penny dropped. The driver thought she had said 'wee old dears' – his usual term of reference for the ladies who catch his bus to the bingo.

AT the door of Morrison's supermarket in Partick, two wifies were having a blether before facing the foul weather outside. It allowed one of them to tell her old pal, 'Aye, ah had tae go to the doacter's efter Christmas because of pains in ma stomach. He told me it was just wind. "Just wind?" ah told him. "It was just wind that brought doon the Tay Bridge."'

OVERHEARD in a Renfrew hotel bar, where a local enquired about another regular, 'Where's Jimmy tonight?' So his friend told him, 'He's stayin' at home. He's bothered wi' his kidney.' Perplexed, the chap asks, 'But ah thought they gied him a new wan.' 'Aye,' he was told, 'but they gied him wan wi' a stane in it.'

A DOCTOR swears this is true, and who are we to doubt members of the medical profession? He was reminiscing about his early days as a general practitioner in Dundee, when a young lady came in declaring she had a problem with a rabbit inside her most private of places. She may have expressed this in a more demotic term. Confused, and fearing he might have to perform some type of Paul Daniels conjuring trick for which medical school at Edinburgh had not prepared him, he asked for further details about the burrowing rodent. The young lady thought the doctor had gone mad, and repeated that she was worried about 'a ra' bit' about her person.

SOMEONE tries to convince us that a chap in hospital, having to breathe with the help of an oxygen mask, mumbled to a nurse, 'Are my testicles black?' She whipped back the covers and his pyjamas to tell him there was nothing wrong with them. It was then he pulled the mask off to ask again, 'Are my test results back?'

A NURSE who did her training in Liverpool tells us that their meagre student-nurse wages were augmented by gifts of tights, chocolate and food left for them by grateful patients and relatives. One evening, she was sitting at the nurses' station when a woman visitor came over with a meat pie and said, 'Would you eat this up, love?' Delighted by the offer, she and a fellow student scoffed the lot before their benefactor returned and enquired, 'Is me 'usband's pie 'ot yet, dear?'

RETIRING Rutherglen GP Douglas Bremner was recalling the time he gave an elderly patient a prescription for pills and told him that he needed to take one in the morning and one in the evening. A few days later, the patient, looking a bit haggard, returned to the surgery for another appointment. 'How are you getting on with the pills?' asked the doc. 'Not very well,' came the response. 'I'm struggling to stay up to one in the morning to take the night-time pill.'

AN office conversation in Glasgow, where the subject of holidays surfaced. One woman declared that this year she was taking a sick relative to Lourdes. A puzzled young girl at the next desk asked how exactly did cricket help.

GEORGE Bryson of Lanark overheard a chap in a Lanarkshire Tesco who spotted a very pregnant young lady who, despite her condition, was still in the regulation local mode of crop top, pierced navel and low-slung denims. The chap drew his wife's attention to the young lady before telling the missus, 'Ah see she's gaun tae huv a Caesarean.' As he was presumably not known for being an expert in such matters, it made his puzzled wife ask how he knew this. So he answered triumphantly, 'She's had a ring-pull fitted.'

A GLASGOW hospital received a phone call from a woman enquiring after the well-being of a Margaret Watson on Ward 7. She was put through to the ward where a nurse told her, 'Mrs Watson had a comfortable night. She's doing well, and we hope she may go home in the next couple of days.' The caller said how relieved she was, as she had feared it was something much worse. The nurse then asked if it was a relative or a friend who was calling, only to be told, 'Neither – it's Margaret Watson in Ward 7. Nobody tells you anything in here.'

A CHAP in Glasgow received a call from the hospital. It was to tell him that he couldn't have an appointment for a scan until 23 August 2007. 'Will that be morning or afternoon?' he asked politely. 'Do you really need to know just now?' asked the receptionist. 'Well, it's just that I've got the plumber coming in the morning,' he told her.

THEN there was the Scots chap on holiday in Florida who turned up at the doctor's clinic the colour of a poached lobster after foolishly lying in the sun too long. The doctor immediately realised it was a terrible case of sunburn and gave him a bottle of calamine lotion and a packet of Viagra tablets. 'I understand the calamine,' said the puzzled Scot, 'but why the Viagra?' 'Oh, that's to keep the bedsheets off you,' says the doc.

A FEMALE reader in Ayrshire attending her local hospital with cystitis was discussing the problem with the woman sitting next to her, who had a similar complaint. So, our reader mentioned to her

that she had been told cranberry juice was good for what ailed them. After a long pause, the woman asked her, 'Do you drink it or apply it?'

WE'RE assured that the following statement was uttered rather too loudly in the Scottish National Blood Transfusion Service's Glasgow office by one of its more inexperienced female nurses. Addressing a male donor, the red-faced young woman apparently caused a stir by gasping, 'No, no! What I meant to say was, "Have you had your thumb pricked?"'

WHAT about the chap who walked into a Glasgow dentist's surgery and told the tooth-puller, 'Excuse me, can you help me? I think I'm a moth.' The puzzled chap in the white coat told him, 'You don't need a dentist. You need a psychiatrist.' When the chap agreed that this was the case, the dentist asked, 'So why did you come in here?' And the chap said, 'Well . . . the light was on.'

WE hear of a Glasgow chap going for a colonoscopy who obviously thought that humour was the best way of dealing with such a delicate and potentially embarrassing situation. Apparently, he told the medical staff, 'Can you write a note for the wife confirming that my head is not, in fact, up there?'

A NEWS report reaches us from America where a patient was diagnosed as clinically depressed and was scheduled for controversial shock therapy until it was discovered that he was not in fact depressed – merely Scottish. Doctors had described him as suffering from Pervasive Negative Anticipation – a belief that everything will turn out for the worst, whether it's trains arriving late, Scotland's chances at winning any international sporting event, or even his own prospects of getting ahead in life and realising his dreams. The doctor treating him explained: 'His story of a childhood growing up in the drab backstreets of a windswept, grey town with treeless streets of identical run-down houses where it rained every day, passionately backing a football team who never won, seemed to be an idealised depressive memory – I thought all that was a myth.' However, identifying the patient as Scottish changed the diagnosis from 'clinical depression' to 'rather quaint and charming'.

TWENTY-SIX

Bouncing along

IF ever there was proof that Glasgow men secretly think they are God's gift to women, it is their dismissal of any club which attracts women older than 30 as 'grab-a-granny' night. But the women are hitting back. When an ageing Lothario approached a young lady at a club and asked her if she thought her equally young blonde pal would fancy a dance with him, she curtly replied, 'Behave yersel'. It's a lumber she wants – no' a pal for her faither.' Equally, a middle-aged reader recalls attending the Savoy, Glasgow's doyen of sticky-carpet nightlife venues, for some grab-a-granny entertainment after an office night out. The dinner-jacketed doormen looked dubiously at our man's colleague, who was swaying slightly. 'Have you been drinking?' the bull-necked steward asked suspiciously. 'Of course I have,' came the honest answer. 'Why else would I want to get in here?' Allan Mackintosh and a group of Glasgow Uni rugby players once arrived at the Savoy on a student night. The stewards eyed up the boisterous players and asked if they had drunk a lot before arriving. Unwisely perhaps, one player immediately blurted out, 'Buckets.' There was a short silence, and then the steward announced, 'I don't blame you, given what's in there tonight.'

QUEUING for entry to a nightclub, reader Robert Kirkwood once received the Glasgow bouncer's all-purpose knock-back, 'Sorry, pal, regulars only the night.' Says Robert: 'The bouncer didn't seem bothered by the fact the group of people he'd just admitted, to whom we'd just spent ten minutes chatting, were over on holiday from Russia. Worse, the club – The Tunnel – had only been open for three days.'

MAKING a rare visit to Glasgow's city centre, two women of advanced years chose to follow a drunken karaoke session in the Horseshoe Bar by tottering across the road to Truffles lapdance emporium. The women's poor chances of entry were much reduced by their frankly scornful manner towards the place's bouncers, beginning with derisive cackles when told entry cost £25. The duo's honest feminism undid them eventually, however. 'We want to come in for a dance,' said one woman. Added her pal, 'And to give the men inside a row.'

SOME Glasgow bouncers are apparently taking courses in diplomacy. Another drink-impaired woman of a certain age was flattered to be refused entry to a club by a doorman who smoothly told her, 'I'm sorry, madam, but you don't fit our standard client-group profile.'

A FORMER bouncer at long-lost Glasgow nightclub Charlie Parker's recalls a variation on the joint's unwritten, somewhat un-PC law: 'Nae ugly burdz, nae fat burdz.' He remembers a special greeting for any unlucky lady who was neither thin nor braw: 'The main bar's full, I'm afraid – perhaps you'd care to have a drink in the Bonne Auberge restaurant downstairs.' This ploy worked well – the Bonne Auberge bar only had two seats – until the night a Charlie Parker waitress found her special guest had been sent downstairs. 'What,' she raged, 'are you trying to say about my mother?'

GLASGOW's long-defunct Henry Afrikas nightclub staged an early gig by Lloyd Cole and the Commotions. As Tom Rafferty recalls, 'To the band's evident chagrin, they were introduced as Lloyd Cole and the Commodores. The bar special that night was Tia Maria. As I recall, it was 29p for the cheapest way to drink Tia Maria – Tia Maria with milk. I realised I'd become an old buffer when I found myself boasting to my daughter about having a night's total debauchery on £3.50 – with enough still left for the late bus home.'

GLASGOW nightclub knock-backs. We hear of one middle-aged business type who staggered out of the Hilton hotel after an awards dinner in his bow tie and dinner suit and asked the taxi driver to take him to a nightclub. The driver deposited him outside the youth-oriented Archaos, where he approached the doorman, who put up a steadying hand and told him, 'Sorry, sir. It's student night tonight.' And through his drink-befuddled thought processes, our chap blurted out, 'It's OK, my good man, I'm studying for my MBA.'

A PENSIONER entered a barber's shop in Glasgow's working-class Partick and, as he had very little on top, it took only a few minutes for his haircut. Now, the shop had a very reasonable £1.50 offer for OAPs but even that did not suit the customer, who complained loudly that the shop was bleeding pensioners dry and should charge even less when they had so little to cut. That gave Stan, the no-nonsense proprietor, the chance to use the line, 'It's not £1.50 to cut it, it's £1.50 to find it.' At that, the grumbling OAP paid up.

READER Andy Render was on a morning shuttle flight to Heathrow when, as the breakfasts were being handed out, one chap looked at his foil container and said, 'I've got bacon.' His wife looked at her container and remarked, 'Well, I've got sausage and egg, but I would prefer bacon. Can you ask if I can change it?' However, when the stewardess was summoned, she insisted that everyone was being served sausage and egg and there was no bacon. The indignant husband insisted he had bacon and, to prove the point, showed her the top of the container. She then explained tactfully that a cooked rasher wasn't in fact steaming away temptingly beneath a silver-foil lid bearing the legend 'ba.com'.

SOMEONE who perhaps should not become a bus driver is the chap in Perth who was sitting his driving test. Beside him in the car, the inspector could see no suitable car nearby with a number plate for the chap to read in order to test his eyesight. So the inspector pointed to the low-bridge sign just ahead and asked him to read it instead. 'Fourteen inches,' replied the wannabe driver. 'I don't think so,' said the inspector. 'Well, it's 14 something,' said the driver, perhaps indicating his Highway Code reading was not up to scratch.

RUEFULLY shaking her head, a vintage rock 'n' roller relates a sad tale of contemporary Glasgow. Her teenage daughter recently went to the theatre with a pal to see Buddy Holly's musical stage biography, *Buddy*. 'That was absolutely brilliant,' her daughter beamed afterwards, becoming aware her friend was racked with tears. 'I thought it was great an' all,' the pal sobbed, 'but why did they have to spoil it with that ending?'

AT the conclusion of every summer, Highland tourist offices' staff compile their list of the public's oddest requests. Rod Johnston, supervisor at the Fort William information centre, says his favourite query was, 'Where can we see the launching of the trees?' After some skilful probing, staff were able to deduce that the German couple concerned were wanting to see caber tossing at a Highland Games. For some unfathomable reason, another tourist-office worker found much mirth in the query, 'Where are the gay bars in Inverness?'

OVERHEARD in Marks & Spencer in Glasgow's Argyle Street, an old dear becoming slightly confused while seeking thick hosiery. Mind you, her request may yet prove a vote winner for the Tories, who are always keen to attract the grey voter: the woman requested 'income support tights'.

READER Jim McGrane was watching Pat Kenny's chat show on Irish TV when an item came on about the Republic's new driving laws. A police spokesperson explained that drivers must now carry their licences at all times when driving. Furthermore, no mobile phones were allowed in cars, plus there'd be more speed controls and a new points penalty system for driving offences. The spokesperson summarised the laudable rationale behind these safety measures: 'It's so those people who died on the roads last year won't die on the roads next year.'

A GLASGOW southside family chose to undertake a bracing Sunday-afternoon stroll through the chilly, frosted whiteness of Queen's Park before taking tea with friends in Strathbungo. As the extreme cold began to bite, the family's eight-year-old son introduced an unexpected air of anticipation to what was scheduled as a rather douce formal gathering: 'Dad, when we get there, will their sexual heating be switched on?'

PROVING just what a desirable tourist spot Glasgow is, the

Glasgow Hilton hotel's website has a section for 'Recreation', listing the distance to various attractions. It states: beach, 25 miles; jet-skiing, 25 miles; pool table, ½ mile; squash, 8 miles; video arcade, 1 mile.

VEGETARIANISM had sparked off a heated debate in a Clydebank local. Finally, one of the regulars taking part blurted out, 'Red meat is definitely not bad for you.' But after a thoughtful pause, he added, 'Now greeny, smelly meat – that's bad for you.'

MEDIA speculation about Michael Jackson's fiscal ill health failed to inspire much sympathy from two travellers on Glasgow's No. 20 bus to Drumchapel. One was explaining the moonwalking former Motown star's wrath over such newspaper allegations, adding, 'Michael was so raging he ordered his plastic surgeon to put an angry look on his face.'

ITALIAN cruise line Costa Crociere offers passengers the chance to make mobile phone calls while at sea. Considering they'll be charged £2.70 a minute, it's fitting that the first ship to offer the service will be the Costa Fortuna.

PERSONAL

HARD WORKING country loving widow seeks middle aged traditional working farmer with farm house for relationship. Please send picture of farmhouse. Please reply to Box No. 6875, The Scottish Farmer, 200 Renfield Street, Glasgow G2 3QB

TWENTY-SEVEN

Sad farewells

ONE of the sadder aspects of chronicling life in Scotland is the passing of people whose lives touched the hearts of many. The end of warm-hearted family entertainment seemed to be signalled by the death of entertainer Rikki Fulton. In sport, folk fondly remembered how Ally McLeod brought a passion to Scottish football rarely seen since; and we recall how Roy Jenkins, in his Glasgow Hillhead parliamentary campaign, showed that being witty, erudite and a wine-drinker was no hindrance to a political career. Today's politicians who are always worrying about putting a foot wrong, please take note.

RIKKI Fulton was a thoughtful friend of The Diary and always willing to phone and tell a story against himself or simply to add a welcome comment to a story that took his fancy. When The Diary asked Rikki what he thought of Edinburgh councillor Paul Nolan, who declared that the west of Scotland humour of Francie and Josie was a poor choice of show at Edinburgh's newly opened Festival Theatre, Rikki cheerily declared, 'He promised he would come to the show with an open mind. I don't mind telling you

there was a helluva draft that night.' And when he was asked how his memorable comic creation, the Rev. I.M. Jolly, popped the question to his dragon-like wife Ephasia, Rikki solemnly said, 'It was a misunderstanding, actually. They had gone for a fish tea at the Ritz Fish and Chicken Bar and afterwards, as she helped him into his taxi, he mumbled, "I'll give you a ring sometime." The magistrate ruled that a definite proposal had been made.'

PAYING tribute to Rikki Fulton at his funeral, Tony Roper recalled a lengthy period which he and Gregor Fisher once spent working together, struggling heroically to write a comedy script. After much effort, the script was as good as the duo felt they could make it, and so they took it to Rikki for his informed opinion. Having read their work, Rikki paused, wearing a thoughtful look on his face. 'The alternative, of course,' Rikki eventually said, 'is that you could play it for laughs.'

A JOURNALIST tells us that one of the joys of covering Ayr United when Ally McLeod was boss after the dark days of

Argentina was the post-match press conferences when Ally held court for hours using pies, biscuits, glasses and drinks bottles to represent players as he explained what had happened during the game. Ally would also defend to the hilt the Scottish squad he took to the World Cup in Argentina, despite press accusations of booze-fuelled binges. Our man with the typewriter tells us, 'Ally would always say that 14 or 15 of the 22 players were teetotal – the rest did the drinking for them.' And when Ally received the telegram at the team's hotel about squad player Willie Johnston's failed drugs test, he went to see the team doctor, Dr Fitzsimmons, a devout Catholic, about it. Ally would recollect, 'He read it, then said, "Ally, there's only one thing you can do now – you'd better get down on your knees with me, for we're going to need all the help we can get."'

FOLK singer Matt McGinn's admirers kept the Calton anarchist's memory alive by performing his songs in New York on Tartan Day. They were supported by folk legend Pete Seeger, who first exposed Matt's talents to the US in 1962 by putting him on at Carnegie Hall. Matt's fee of $200 was $140 more than was paid to another Seeger protégé on that night's bill, a young unknown called Bob Dylan. Before the gig, Bob became nervous about his readiness to play guitar, enquiring, 'Hey, Matt, you got any nail clippers?' Unsurprisingly, Matt didn't, confining himself to the curt observation, 'Very few Glasgow men carry them around with them.'

PARENTAL support was vital during the long genesis of *This Turbulent Priest*, Stephen McGinty's biography of Cardinal Thomas Winning. Stephen revealed that the book's unfinished state was a topic of family discussion on the night of the cardinal's sudden and untimely demise. Sensing Stephen's personal and professional grief, his father, Frank, sought to console him. 'Ah, well, Stephen,' Frank said after a moment's consideration. 'At least you know now how the book ends.'

VETERAN Hollywood actor Jack Elam always took a pragmatic view of his professional status. Long before his recent death, the ubiquitous Western baddie summarised the five distinct stages of his film-acting career as: '1. Who the hell's Jack Elam? 2. Get me Jack Elam! 3. Get me a Jack Elam type. 4. Get me a young Jack Elam. 5. Who the hell's Jack Elam?'

POLITICS in Scotland seems duller since the late Roy Jenkins was a Glasgow MP. Partick Thistle-fan Jonathan Kennedy recalls that soon after Roy was elected in Hillhead he was invited, as the local MP, to Firhill by the then Jags chairman, Miller Reid. It was a particularly dull affair against Hibs, and, after about 20 minutes, Roy asked Miller, 'Which way are Thistle shooting?' Miller politely told Roy that Thistle were the team in red and yellow. 'I know that,' said Roy, 'but which way are they shooting?'

A READER insists that, driving through Lancashire, he heard a local commercial radio station misjudge the tone of its heartfelt salute to the recently deceased Bee Gee, Maurice Gibb. As the Gibb brothers' falsetto harmonies faded out, the DJ apparently said, 'Staying Alive . . . Maurice Gibb . . . but sadly in his case not forever.'

SOMETIMES *The Herald*'s thoughtful obituaries page is missed by readers in a hurry. So we pass on from the obituary of Brigadier Sir Gregor MacGregor of MacGregor a vignette from his time as Officer Commanding (Lowland Brigade). And we quote: 'A competent horseman, he was passing in front of the band when his mount noisily broke wind. "Sorry about that, Brigade of Drums," he called. "That's all right, sir," replied a piper. "We thought it was the horse."'

FOLLOWING his sudden death, cheerfully avuncular man-of-music Neville Garden is sorely missed at the BBC. A friend at the Beeb tells us: 'On one memorable occasion, Neville had been invited to attend the Gaels' annual festival of music and culture, the National Mod. And with great relish, he announced over the airwaves that he would certainly be going along. 'I can't possibly refuse the invitation,' he said, adding memorably, 'I may never have the opportunity again to use the phrase, "Come into the Mod, Garden."'

OUR mention in The Diary of the late Zimbabwean president the Revd Canaan Banana reminded Murray Macmillan of staging a general-knowledge quiz in his workplace in Falkirk. Competition for team places was so keen that trials were held. One young woman was determined to be chosen, but struggled throughout. Near the end, she was asked, 'Who was the first president of Zimbabwe?' Clearly toiling, she was offered a clue: 'Think of a fruit.' The girl's face lit up as she firmly responded, 'Max Jaffa.'

THE late Hollywood hard man Charles Bronson holidayed near Mallaig 20 years ago with wife Jill Ireland, choosing the Marine Hotel for lunch. Locals were used to Burt Lancaster and Fulton McKay being about filming Local Hero. They were unsure, however, whether this really was Charles Bronson. As the public bar's clock ticked, the regulars sized up Bronson, while Bronson stared intently back. Fisherman Peter McLean finally broke the silence, demanding the barman's pen and notepad. Scrawling his nickname – Poopsie – Peter strode up to the Death Wish star with a sheet of paper, saying, 'Here, this will save you asking me for my autograph.'

FOLK group Capercaillie's Donald Shaw well remembers the generosity of deceased folk star Johnny Cunningham, brother of Phil, during the band's first trip to America. Scots émigré Johnny collected them at Boston airport and took them home for a meal during which Donald asked Johnny whether after ten years in the States he ever felt like returning home. Johnny admitted he missed certain things, but said he'd been lucky in finding a local butcher who sold Scotch pies. 'Whenever I'm really homesick,' said Johnny, 'I stand in the shower with the water running cold, eating a Scotch pie, remembering why I left.'

THE death of film great Marlon Brando reminds us of the BBC Scotland researcher working on the series *Hollywood Greats* who telephoned an American number which he had been told was an answering service to pass on a message to Brando. However, it was the man himself who answered, understandably in a woozy voice, as it was the middle of the night. But despite his reputation for being difficult, Brando merely asked the researcher to prove he worked for BBC Scotland by saying, 'Braw bricht moonlicht nicht'.

TWENTY-EIGHT

A funny old game

SCOTLAND is not just a footballing nation, as every week thousands strive to hit the perfect golf shot, roll the best bool, or foolishly play for the former-pupils rugby side. But even at its most serious, there is humour to be hacked out of even the worst sporting experience. Scotland's Grand Slam rugby captain, David Sole, recalls playing in a pro-am at Gleneagles with former Open champion Nick Faldo when he hit a wayward shot at the 16th. Trying to joke about it, David turned to his caddie, remarking, 'Golf's a funny old game.' The wizened bag-carrier agreed, before adding, 'But it's no' meant to be, surr.'

ATTENDING a formal dinner packed with bankers and corporate lawyers, a self-made Glasgow construction-industry boss soon felt uncomfortable. The builder found himself sitting next to a stuffy old cove who half-heartedly quizzed him on his holiday plans. 'We've a family caravan we get away to in St Andrews,' said the builder. 'Ah, St Andrews – up there a lot?' asked the old chap, suddenly showing more interest. 'Actually, we've been in St Andrews so often we're going to take out membership,' the builder said. 'The Royal and Ancient?' came the eager enquiry. 'No,' the builder replied, 'Global Video.'

THE Merrylea Parish church website tells us that one of the church elders was torn between attending Sunday's morning service and a rescheduled golf match. Phoning the minister to apologise for his absence, he explained, 'Sorry, but I won't be able to make it tomorrow morning as I'm spending a few hours with some handicapped people.' The website also cheers us up with the story of the wee boy who told the minister after the service that when he grew up he would give him some money. The minister, thanking him for thinking so charitably, then enquired what had prompted this Christian act. 'Because my dad says you are the poorest minister we've ever had,' replied the boy.

WE hear of a stag party from Glasgow which had clay-pigeon shooting down near Manchester as part of its itinerary. As the chaps were extremely hungover, the shooting was not up to scratch. One lad, perhaps worried about a gun going off so near his fragile head, seemed loath to loose his weapon. After the fourth clay pigeon had sailed past his stand without a shot being fired, the assistant manning the catapult asked him, 'Are you waiting for them to perch?'

THE Ardrossan to Arran ferry was very busy one Friday with folk looking for some rest and recreation on the island. One lady, apparently from Glasgow's West End, had a golf bag with expensive Calloway clubs plus a large bunch of lilies sticking out of it. Halfway across, a fellow traveller could stand it no longer. 'What sort of distance do you get from them?' he enquired innocently.

A CARNOUSTIE golfer called Jack was back from a golfing trip to Florida and was telling pals that he played a round with a local who greeted him with a smile, a warm handshake, and the words, 'Hi, I'm Jack.' Our Carnoustie chap replied, 'Snap' and was therefore taken by surprise when he played a neat chip out of a bunker at the first to be told, 'Great shot, Snap!'

WHEN ex-Ranger Ally McCoist met rugby's John Beattie at a charity dinner in Glasgow, he asked him, 'I've always wanted to know, John, does the London side Wasps have a B Team?'

A DOUGHTY member of the women's darts team at the Stag's Head in Dumbarton was selling raffle tickets when she approached a non-regular and asked him, 'Huv ye had a shot, son?' Clearly having taken his brave pills, he replied, 'I don't know. But your face is familiar.'

RUGBY internationalist Sean Lineen joked that once on a tour of New Zealand, fellow internationalist Gavin Hastings was upset when there was no bacon left when he went down for breakfast and told the waitress, 'What, with all those sheep around here?'

WE hear from Kilmacolm Golf Club where a number of the more elderly members have been fitted with hip and knee replacements. This allowed one member to declare in the bar, 'There is now more titanium in the members than there is in their golf bags.' And when one such recipient declared, 'My doctor says I'll be able to play golf in a matter of weeks,' the cynic at the bar immediately retorted, 'That's amazing, considering you haven't been able to play for the past 30-odd years.'

READER Jim Morrison was playing bowls in Paisley when he heard one of the opposition team being called Saddam by his teammates. He thought that was perhaps a bit of a cruel nickname, even if the chap did bear a slight resemblance to the deposed dictator. However, he was later told by the chap's teammates it was not because of any physical appearance, but due to the fact that the chap, whenever a shot went wrong, always said, 'Atsadamn shame.'

PROOF perhaps that lawn bowls is still for the more mature among us comes from Mount Vernon Bowling Club and its application to Glasgow Licensing Board for a regular extension to its drinks licence. The reason given to the board was for match fixtures and members' funerals.

FORMER Scotland rugby star Eric Peters managed to slip one over the old enemy when taking part in a BBC radio discussion on how players spend their time between games in the Rugby World Cup. Eric stated that he recalled an English front-row – historically not the brightest of chaps – who said they were going for a game of bridge. Eric thought he couldn't miss it, and watched them deal out the cards. Then, said Eric, whenever two cards the same were played, the players tried to be the quickest to slap their hand down on top of them and shout, 'Bridge!'

SCOTTISH Athletics, the official organisation that looks after our runners, has a noticeboard on its website for folk to write in their views. And just to keep it clean, it has what's called a 'profanity filter' to stop bad words appearing. All was going well until famous coach Frank Dick was appointed to lead Scotland's Commonwealth Games squad. Whenever anyone wrote about him on the Scottish Athletics website, it came up as 'Frank Thingy'. The profanity filter, we are told, has now been adjusted.

WE hear of a golfer beginning his pre-shot routine at a busy course. He was visualising the upcoming shot when a piercing voice came over the clubhouse speaker: 'Would the gentleman on the women's tee move back to the men's tee please.' Deep in his routine, the golfer was seemingly impervious to the interruption. Again, the announcement: 'Would the MAN on the WOMEN'S tee kindly move back to the men's tee.' The golfer grew agitated, but decided to continue, only to snap when a third identical announcement boomed across the golf course. 'Would the a*** in the clubhouse kindly shut up and let me play my second shot,' he retorted.